Inspirational Management

Inspirational Management

Sylvia Nash
Chief Executive Officer of the Christian Management Association

MOODY PRESS

CHICAGO

ISBN: 0-8024-3989-6

1 3 5 7 9 10 8 6 4 2

Printed in the United States of America

Inspirational Management

Sylvia Nash

Chief Executive Officer of the
Christian Management Association

MOODY PRESS

CHICAGO

ISBN: 0-8024-3989-6

1 3 5 7 9 10 8 6 4 2

Printed in the United States of America

Contents

Personnel—Motivation

Sex Roles

Ethics

Serving

God in the Workplace

Foreword

In my judgment few people are better qualified to write on the subject of the manager and his or her role in effectively serving the Lord than Sylvia Nash.

Sylvia and I have worked closely together for a number of years in the ministry of the Christian Management Association, she as our executive director and CEO, and I as a member, presently chairman, of the board.

Thus, I have witnessed her putting these practical suggestions to work in her own ministry and recognize that she is a careful, successful practitioner as well as a teacher.

In this fine presentation are practical, helpful, workable suggestions for every person in the marketplace, at whatever level of responsibility he may find himself. Sylvia reminds us that Christians need to bring Christian values to bear upon our day-to-day responsibilities in the workplace. She helps us to see that what God teaches us in the quiet places and moments serves us well, if we allow it to, in the daily management tasks.

Each section of this book is a jewel in itself. Don't try to read it in one sitting. Take a section at a time, absorb it, put it to practice, and then move on to the next area.

Here is down-to-earth advice garnered out of a varied—and eminently successful—managerial career. Here is not only theory but practical reality.

This is a biblically oriented handbook that you will want to share with colleagues and associates. Use it for dialogue; discuss the issues that Sylvia presents. Everyone will benefit from such an experience.

This book runs the gamut of managerial challenges from "Conflict in the Workplace" to avoiding boredom to "Dressing for Success" to "Dealing with Sexual Harassment" to handling interruptions to good use of the telephone and on and on.

Sylvia understands that management is both a science and an art. She treats both aspects of this role with sensitivity and from a scriptural perspective.

All of us will be better managers if we heed even a portion of this sound advice. Enjoy.

TED W. ENGSTROM
President Emeritus
World Vision

Introduction:
Fundamental Principles

The pilot reports to the passengers, "Well, folks, we have some good news and some bad news. The bad news is that our navigation and communications systems are out, so we don't know where we are or which way we're going. The good news is that we are making excellent time."

An old joke, but it reminds me how much of good management boils down to careful attention to a few basic principles: knowing where you are, where you want to go, and how to get there.

Knowing Where You Are

Where are you as an individual or an organization? What are your strengths and weaknesses? Are you building on your strengths or just trying to overcome weaknesses? Progress is made only by exploiting opportunities, not by just solving problems. If you don't know what you are good at (individually or as an organization), you may take on projects you are ill-suited for.

It's OK if you aren't good at everything. No one is. Find out what your gifts are, and use them.

You have heard it said, "When you're up to your neck in alligators, it's hard to remember that your original purpose was to drain the swamp." If you are in the swamp, maybe you need to climb a tree from time to time. Look around, get some perspective. Getting away for a conference may be a good start.

9

Knowing Where You Are Going

An up-to-date purpose statement is essential. A good statement is specific enough to help you determine where you are going. It also indicates something even more important: you know where you are *not* going. A purpose statement helps you focus on specific goals. It keeps you from attempting the wrong things, from "flying off in all directions."

In forming your mission statement you need to look not only at your strengths as an organization but also at the trends in the outside environment. I heard a story years ago about a television evangelist who invested ministry money in a girdle factory about the time that the invention of pantyhose made girdles unnecessary. Obviously he wasn't paying attention to the outside trends.

Knowing How to Get There

It takes careful planning and discipline to go in a desired direction. Establish policies and procedures so that everyone is operating under the same assumptions. It helps to read your purpose statement regularly, then formulate goals to help you achieve your purpose.

Daily prioritize your activities *in light of your goals.* Spend time on the most important activities. Watch out for "the tyranny of the urgent." Without careful planning, the days quickly fill up with work that seems important, even urgent, but that may have little relationship to your ultimate goals.

Peter Drucker put it well. "The urgent is rarely important, and the important is rarely urgent."

The story is told of a visitor coming upon cellist Pablo Casals as he was practicing scales. The visitor was surprised to find the great cellist doing such simple exercises, but Casals pointed out that playing the cello amounts to just getting from one note to another.

Much success in life, as well as management, comes from paying attention to fundamental, basic principles.

Time Management—
Organization

The Time Trap

The start of each day signals a challenge to all busy executives.

God gave each of us twenty-four hours: that's 1,440 minutes or 86,400 seconds per day. Our watches all run at the same speed. God knew the amount of time we needed to accomplish what He intended each given day. The challenge is to spend our time on the most important priorities.

Ray Ortland, president of Haven of Rest Ministries in Los Angeles, finds that the best way for him to accomplish God's tasks each day is to pray over his "To Do" list. He asks God to bless each appointment, to help him focus on the needs of those he ministers to, and to help him eliminate the unnecessary tasks that could deter him from his business goals. We would do well to commit our time each morning to the Lord and allow Him to be the ruler of the time He has entrusted to us.

Learning to Say No

Sometimes no can be the most difficult word in our vocabulary.

"What will people say?" we argue. "If I don't, who will?" "I'm probably the only one who will get it done properly," "No one else will be able to do it as well as I can"—and the list goes on. If you have trouble saying no, you might try saying, "Thank you for asking me. I am honored. Let me pray about it and see if this will fit into the commitments I have already made." After you have done that, maybe a gracious no in a letter will be easier for you. There is no need to feel pressured into an immediate yes prior to counting the costs.

Learn to say no to items you know should be delegated. Delegating also encourages management growth in others on your team.

Say no to things that will not lead you toward your company goals and further your purpose.

Without an organized system for accomplishing your daily tasks, your life will be filled with chaos and confusion. Many good systems are available. Find one that works best for you.

Have you ever tried going on a diet and felt the struggle for discipline in those early days? I have, and it's hard. It is always difficult to eliminate bad habits or develop good ones—it takes ten to twenty-one days to make or break a habit. Whatever system you decide to use, be sure to begin with the resolve and determination that you will stick with it for ten to twenty-one days. After that, it should be part of your routine that will bring about greater efficiency.

Where Do I Begin?

Begin each day with a "To Do" list. Prioritize each item: A = "Must do," B = "Should do," and C = "Could do." Ask yourself:

1. Is it worth doing?
2. Is it something only I can do?
3. Is it a top priority—a "must do" item?

Begin by dealing with only the "A" items. When you have completed those, proceed to the "B" items, and so on.

Don't waste time in unnecessary meetings. Attend only the meetings where you are absolutely needed. Watch the time you spend on the phone. You may want a stopwatch to help you monitor yourself if that is a problem for you.

Do your creative work at a time of the day when you are at your best. Discover your energy curve. For me, it is the morning hours. At about 1:30 in the afternoon, my energy

14

starts to take a dip. Try to reserve that slow time for "phone backs" or other projects that don't require high concentration.

Select optimum energy times to meet with your colleagues. Maybe your team members find the early morning hours to be an intrusive time and difficult for them to be alert and creative. If so, change your staff meetings to times better suited to all your energy needs.

Interruptions are part of life, like it or not. The average manager is interrupted two hundred times a day—every six to nine minutes. So schedule one to two hours each day for interruptions. It will lesson your anxiety to know that your entire schedule won't be thrown off by an unexpected call or visitor.

However, you may be inadvertently inviting extra interruptions. Does your desk face the door so that everyone feels encouraged to visit with you as they pass? Do you have a candy dish filled with chocolates that scream to be eaten by everyone entering your office? What causes interruptions in your day? There may be things you can do to cut down on unwanted intrusions.

Commit your day to the Lord each morning as you rise. Repent of things you should not be doing, and ask God to direct you to the plans He has for you each sunrise. That will allow you to tackle the tasks in the time He has given you.

Got a Second?

How many times a day do you hear the words "Got a second?" Leaders have a constant challenge each day to guard against costly interruptions while remaining available to those who report to us.

The "open door" and "closed door" policies have been widely debated. I much prefer the "open door." An opened door signals to co-workers that "You are important" and that "Your project is important." If I am tackling a task that requires deep concentration, then I either work away from the office or with my door closed.

When trust is built so that your colleagues know they can have easy access and quick responses from you, they will be understanding when on occasion their request for "a second" needs to be postponed.

I saw a sign once that read, "Artist at work! I'm planning to be creative until 3:00 P.M., but please don't let me miss your idea." The lighthearted message gets the point across.

All too often "a second" can amount to a half hour or more. Ask for a more realistic time frame, and then propose, "Let's give it our all for the next twenty-five minutes and then reschedule more time later if we need it."

Commissioner Kenneth Hodder of the Salvation Army explained his routine for guarding against those precious "seconds." He has a starting and stopping time for all appointments, which usually go for no more than thirty minutes. After twenty-five minutes, he announces that five minutes remain and suggests that they use that time for any final details.

"If further discussion is needed, my secretary will be happy to reschedule another thirty-minute meeting." That approach discourages excessive small talk and encourages those meeting with him to be organized in their meeting time.

These are things we can do to guard against excessive requests for "a second":

- Position your office furniture so that it isn't an open invitation to interruptions.
- Agree with your colleagues to respect one another's "quiet times" through agreed upon signals, such as a closed door.
- Pile important looking papers in the extra chair that can easily be removed if you want time with a colleague.
- Guard against too much casual office conversation as it can undermine your schedule. "I'd love to hear the whole story over lunch" is an effective way of coping.
- Schedule meetings in others' offices so that you can feel free to leave at the appropriate time.
- "Concluding comments" to summarize your discussion will help you end the conversation.
- State at the onset of the meeting how much time you have so that the parameters are clearly defined. As the time to finish approaches, gently restate that you need to conclude in five minutes.

No matter how busy we are, our Lord is never too busy to listen to us or answer our cries to Him. He says, "Come to me, all you who are weary and burdened, and I will give you rest" (Matthew 11:28). He commands us, "Call to me and I will answer you" (Jeremiah 33:3). What a comforting promise!

Planning Beyond the Moment

Would you begin a vacation without first checking the map and making general plans as to where you are going and how long it will take to get there? Planning ahead is the only way to reach your goal.

Successfully completed projects are usually a team effort. Great projects and programs don't just happen. They come through hard work on the part of many people.

Lack of proper planning can produce chaos, confusion, and conflict. It opens the door for unnecessary errors and possible embarrassment and can produce disastrous consequences. Such was the case on August 21, 1991, when word came of the attempted coup in Moscow. Ninety-six hours later, Mr. Gorbachev was released and the coup had failed.

Improper planning was evident. We saw what happens when events are not planned carefully: lack of unity, lack of support, indecision, lack of definitive orders, no clear sense of purpose, and miscalculation of the strength and courage of the opposition. Proverbs 11:14 says, "For lack of guidance a nation falls, but many advisers make victory sure."

Proper planning requires:

- Unity and commitment from the entire team
- A common goal and purpose
- A willingness to listen to all members of the team and to value their input
- Clearly spelled out job duties and responsibilities
- Knowledge of purpose and objectives

- Access to pertinent facts and necessary research
- A time frame with regular check-in points to keep the entire team on schedule
- A willingness to change or modify objectives, strategies, and plans when necessary
- Creativity and new ideas
- Approval and review from all members of the team so that changes, corrections, or additions can be made prior to completion
- A willingness to share the praise and the blame with the entire team

I believe the Lord helps us in our planning. We need to do our best and then ask God for His guidance and direction. Luke 14:28 states, "Suppose one of you wants to build a tower. Will he not first sit down and estimate the cost to see if he has enough money to complete it?" In that passage the Lord is encouraging us to be deliberate and systematic in our efforts.

When Meetings Go On and On

The May 1985 issue of *Personnel Journal* states that the most costly communication activity in any organization is the internal business meeting. Maybe you haven't thought of meetings in terms of cost, but consider twelve to fourteen well-paid individuals around a conference table for about two hours. The cost of one session? Approximately $1,000. Think further of the number of meetings held each week in your business and multiply that by fifty-two weeks per year and $1,000 per session. The figure is staggering, isn't it?

How often have you left a meeting saying, "That was a waste of time"? How often has your participation been unnecessary to accomplish the goals of the meeting? Meetings do not have to be a waste of time and money if they solve problems or develop personnel.

I served on a board some years ago that met monthly. It was a board known for continuing far into the night. I knew that I was not even coherent at midnight and would certainly not be able to make intelligent decisions on behalf of the ministry at that time. When I agreed to join the board, I explained that I would be leaving at 10:00 P.M. whether or not the meeting agenda was completed. That began a new trend for the ministry. The board became successful at completing its meetings by 10:00 P.M. rather than midnight or 1:00 A.M.

Has your organization set forth policies or guidelines that can help ensure that your meetings are productive?

If you find yourself spending a lot of time in meetings that run on too long and accomplish little, these suggestions might be helpful:

1. Only invite those who are directly responsible for the issues at hand.
2. Start your meetings at an odd time, such as 9:28 instead of 9:30, to indicate exact starting time.
3. Start and end your meetings on time.
4. Consider a "stand up" staff meeting with no coffee or chairs. This will facilitate much shorter meetings, help cut through the small talk, and accomplish more in less time.
5. If a meeting tends to drag on too long, schedule it just before another appointment, right before lunch, or just prior to closing time. Your meeting is more likely to end on time.
6. Have prepared agendas for all meetings.
7. Indicate a time schedule and person responsible for each agenda item.
8. When you set up a room for a large meeting, put three or four rows of plush seats in front with the harder seats behind them. That will help fill the front of the room first and encourage attendees to come early to get the best seats.
9. If you get bogged down on one topic, assign someone to study it further and report back to the group at a later date.
10. Request a brief written report and proposed recommendations on each agenda item. The person responsible for the item is thus "forced" to come prepared with research, facts, and proposed steps for the group to take—hence hastening the process and shortening the meeting.
11. Send out a summary or minutes within seventy-two hours of the meeting so that items needing action can be acted upon quickly.
12. Indicate in the minutes who is responsible for follow-through on each agenda item.
13. Have a quick review at the next meeting to ensure accountability and follow-through for action items.

Dealing with Interruptions

"If I get one more interruption, I'll scream!"

Those words rang out one day as one of the staff expressed her frustration at the constantly ringing phone. Someone else shot back, "If you don't get any more phone calls, you won't get paid." Sometimes we forget that our "interruptions" are the very reason we were hired.

Students sometimes call my college professor husband at awkward times, but I have to try to remember that answering questions from students is part of what he is paid to do.

There are times, however, when an interruption during a creative session can cause irreparable damage. Someone distracts you just as the light begins to dawn on the solution to a thorny problem, and it can be hours before you recapture the thought, if ever. An interruption in the middle of a counseling session can lose the moment forever.

John Molloy, author of *Dress for Success*, had been struggling for months to solve a very difficult problem. He was in a creative session and had finally arrived at the solution. Before he could get it down on paper, however, the phone rang. He stopped to answer it, and the solution was gone forever. To this day, he has no recollection of the solution he had reached.

I've heard it said that the average manager has two hundred separate interruptions per day. They come with the territory. Some reports indicate that they come every six to nine minutes.

What can we do to curb unnecessary interruptions? To begin, it might be an interesting study to evaluate your time blocks for one week. Make a chart with four columns. Jot down the time of each interruption in one column. In the second column note how long it took you to get back to the task. The third column could be used to indicate who or what caused the interruption. Use the final column for any additional comments.

One executive discovered that most of her interruptions were self-inflicted. She had not collected the tools she needed at the start of the project, so every ten to fifteen minutes she had to jump up and retrieve another file, book, or resource guide. Another executive found that 80 percent of what he was doing was secretarial. His tasks could be accomplished by someone else with greater efficiency and for less money.

Your colleagues would be very understanding if you needed special times with no interruptions. A simple sign on the door might be helpful.

SHHHHHHH
Creative
Thinking
Inside.
Out at _____.

A completion time helps other staff members know how long you wish to be alone. If, for example, you plan to be done in fifteen minutes, almost any "emergency" can wait. On the other hand, if you will not be available for two hours, they can judge whether the problem is urgent enough to interrupt you.

I use colored folders with staff names on each folder to help curb my interruption patterns. When I have a question or an item to discuss, I toss it in the folder to wait until my scheduled time with that person. That not only keeps me focused on my work, but it helps the staff to keep focused on their tasks as well.

MacDonald's executives are expected to spend six hours per week at the top floor of their executive building lying on a water bed looking up at the skylight. There are no interruptions, and creativity is allowed to flow.

Interruption reducers:

- Schedule a specific, regular creative/quiet time when you permit no interruptions. People will remember this regular time and respect it.
- Remove the candy dish from your desk. It's an open invitation to interruptions.
- Turn your desk away from the door so you won't have a tendency to look up every time someone passes your office.
- Have meetings in other people's offices rather than yours so that you can control when you want to end the conversation.
- Speak with unexpected callers, such as salespeople, in the reception area where you can remain standing and limit the length of the conversation.
- Have a start and stop time to your meetings.

The bottom line is that you need to take charge of your time. Only you can decide what are interruptions and what are not, and then deal with them accordingly.

The Telephone:
Tool or Terror

To some of us, the telephone is a constant interruption and irritation. Many of us have forgotten that one of our main jobs is using this vital tool to advance the business.

If you are a fund-raiser, a call from a donor is not an interruption. A receptionist who thinks answering the phone is a nuisance has forgotten her primary job. We need to be reminded of the importance of those calls that keep our business alive.

"The telephone," says Donald Hackett, one of America's most highly regarded communications experts, "is probably the most important piece of equipment in today's average office, yet it is also probably the most abused instrument of any organization." And, he adds, "More customers have been lost by companies through unfortunate telephone conversations than any other device in the typical business office."

The average person makes or receives thirty phone calls per day. I'm sure you can track some days when the number is between sixty and ninety. Therefore, it is important for us to organize our time with precision so that each call is effective. We need to be considerate of the caller's time as well as our own. Here are some suggestions:

- Get to the point and purpose for the call as quickly as possible.
- Log your beginning time so that you can track the time you spend on each call.

- List each item that you intend to cover, thereby eliminating the need for a follow-up call to cover forgotten items.
- When you get bogged down, use phrases such as, "How can I help you further?" "Is there anything more I can do for you?" "I have five more minutes before my next commitment—can we wrap this up in that time or should we reschedule for another time?"
- Calendar your commitments and promises, that is, "I'll get you that report by Friday." Your word of honor needs to be maintained.
- If telephone tag is eating up your day, consider returning your calls ten minutes before noon or ten minutes before 5:00 P.M. Most people are in their offices at those times.
- If you have a tendency to go on and on with your conversations, begin to use a stopwatch as a reminder to be brief and to the point.
- If return calls are necessary, make sure you indicate times when you are and are not available or ask what time would be convenient to return the call.
- If you need to call people who have a tendency to go on and on, begin your conversation with "I have five items to talk about with you."
- If you find it hard to find study time, establish a "hold-all-calls" period at a regular time each day, such as 9:00-11:00 A.M.

Train Your Support Staff

Don't assume that your assistant knows how you want your calls handled. Take the necessary time to train and retrain to avoid embarrassment for you, your assistant, and your organization.

Recently I made a call where the individual answering the phone said, "Oh, no, he isn't in at this time of the day—it's only 8:15, and he never gets in until about 9:30 or 10:00."

I'm certain the boss did not know his call was being answered in that manner. A simple "He (or she) is away from the office at this time" is far more professional and does not leave the caller with an opportunity to make judgments about the executive's schedule. Listen to what is being said. Call the office yourself, and monitor how customers are being treated.

One senior pastor called his church long distance and was left on hold, unattended for thirty minutes. Can you imagine how he felt? How would a customer or a church member feel?

The receptionist is the most important public relations person in your organization. Many times it is the only voice in your company that people will ever hear. Answering the phone with enthusiasm and a desire to serve is crucial.

When your receptionist or assistant places a call on hold, be sure he or she returns to the caller every thirty seconds or so to reassure him that he has not been forgotten. Music while on hold is helpful in assuring the caller that he or she has not been disconnected. The music should not be unpleasant to callers in volume or type.

If It's Not in Writing, It Doesn't Exist

Many telephone discussion items need to be confirmed in writing to avoid misunderstanding. Hundreds of dollars can be saved by logging telephone calls and making brief notes of conversations, and also by written confirmations to ensure that verbal information was received correctly. In some cases, your logged notes may be proof when a difference of opinion arises.

The telephone doesn't have to be an irritation if used efficiently. It can become music to your ear once you have taken control of it and are regarding it as an effective business tool.

The Tyranny of the Trivial

A person doesn't sit down one day and say, "I think I will put on an extra twenty pounds." Gaining weight is a process of several small decisions that eventually result in twenty pounds of extra weight.

Some of life's really large decisions, such as getting married or buying a house, can be recognized for what they are, because they seem big and important at the time. But sometimes choices that affect us the most sneak up on us. Saving money, losing weight, establishing a daily devotional life, and so on may begin with one big decision, but they are carried through with little decisions on a daily basis.

Marital infidelity rarely begins with a decision to be unfaithful. It starts with the "innocent" flirtation—an unwise phone call, a lingering look, impure thoughts. Grand larceny starts with "borrowing" a couple of bucks from petty cash.

Spiritual coldness may come from being too busy to have a quiet time today. Some of us get into regular routines and a break in those routines can stop a good habit. I listen to the Bible on tapes in the morning as I dress for work. But if something interrupts that schedule, it may take me a day or two to get back to it.

My husband and I like to walk. Rainy weather may cause us to skip two or three nights of walking, or a trip out of town can interrupt our discipline, and before long it is really hard to get back into the routine.

"Trivial" decisions often end up being the most important decisions we make. A decision on a busy day to take a whole series of unimportant phone calls can keep you from your "A" priorities. Allowing trivial interruptions to continue for long periods of time can cause your department or organization to flounder.

Many of us are not tempted to sin in big ways, but we succumb to the temptation to do "good" things rather than the best.

Here are some significant decisions you can make today:

- I will focus on the important issues of this day and not allow unnecessary interruptions to rob me of achieving the goals God has for me today.
- I will work to form good habits and keep them.
- I will become more aware of the subtle ways that impropriety begins and deal with it early.
- I will remember that every decision is important and needs to be under the control of God's Spirit in my life.
- As individuals come to mind today, I will consider that a reminder to pray for them and bring them before the throne of grace.
- I will commit myself to completing my "A" priorities and use high energy times to work on the difficult tasks.

"We take captive every thought to make it obedient to Christ" (1 Corinthians 10:5b).

Time Management—
Pressure

Pressures in the Workplace

Have you begun your week with a new zest for life? Are you soaring with the eagles? Have you set new goals to let God use you and fill you with His presence and glory? Are you keeping your mind, soul, and body fully active—running at top speed with Him?

Sometimes we allow our minds to die at an early age. We retire mentally while we still have twenty years of work left. Some people are always going to set the world on fire—tomorrow or next year.

You probably know individuals who are full of ideas about how to "make it big." They are going places. Right to the top. But suddenly they run out of gas, go flat, dry up. They haven't had a new idea in—who knows how long? The only place they go is to the office and back. When they talk, no one listens. Like zombies, they just go through the motions. They appear to be walking in their sleep. Or dead.

When we stop thinking, stop acting creatively, stop finding the excitement in life, we become emotionally and mentally stagnant. Ever wonder why?

Perhaps with the subtle pressures of our marketplace, we have failed to keep our eyes fixed on the Son of God. How easy it is to fall into "the big," "the super," the "better than others" syndrome. But in our "pious" chase for recognition we burn out our motor—even our midnight oil runs out. Prayer times shorten. Reading the Word, once a thrill, becomes routine at best, sometimes extinct. Where once we found freshness of spirit, newness of mind, and fountains of creativity through daily, even hourly, communication with the

Lord Himself—now our inadequacies and lack of energy prevent us from fulfilling even simple goals.

The new week offers us unlimited opportunities to become—and remain—alive. Opportunities to be a vibrant leader, to direct the most important tasks of an organization with adequate (yes, even superior) precision of intellect and execution.

God has given us an incredible example of an alert, active, thinking, and caring mind in His Son. Look to Him to meet all your needs, and you'll be free of the stresses that currently weigh you down. "Those who hope in the Lord will renew their strength. They will soar on wings like eagles; they will run and not grow weary, they will walk and not be faint" (Isaiah 40:31).

You Deserve a Break Today

It is wonderful to return from a vacation and feel refreshed, rejuvenated, and relaxed. Taking a break is important for everyone, not only for health reasons but for spiritual renewal.

As a workaholic, it is hard for me to "come away" as the Lord admonishes us to do, but how vital it is to be refreshed from our labors.

Matthew 11:28-30 says, "Come to me, all you who are weary and burdened, and I will give you rest. Take my yoke upon you and learn from me, for I am gentle and humble in heart, and you will find rest for your souls. For my yoke is easy and my burden is light." Some of us have a tendency to try to carry the weight of the world, but that is not what God intends. His yoke is easy—manageable.

Webster defines rest as "a refreshing quiet, inactivity after exertion or labor, relief or freedom from troubles or exertion, a period or interval of inactivity or tranquillity, mental or spiritual calm."

Rest is necessary to maintain efficiency. Getting away helps us see things from a fresh viewpoint. Sometimes we can see that the project we are poring over is not worth the effort.

Even during our work week we need to take a break now and then. Ted Engstrom recently spoke at a conference of chief executive officers about the importance of taking time out to think, create, and regroup. He encouraged us to think of twenty-one blocks of time each week—seven mornings, seven afternoons, and seven evenings. To keep from compulsive work behavior, we should work no more than fourteen or fifteen blocks per week. That gives us time for the Lord, our families, and personal time. We need to guard our segments of time so that they don't get eaten up without our consent.

Ted additionally suggested that we "block out two hours per day without appointments." Such scheduling is important so that you can be available for creative study time or emergency appointments.

Do you deserve a break today? Take one whether or not you think you do; it will help you become more efficient. Unless Murphy's Law is repealed you won't get everything done anyway, so take a break—then spend the rest of your day doing the important stuff!

Preparing for the End

It was Mother's Day, which meant it was a day off for the women of the Mariner's choir. The men's choir marched in, and Eric Hulst was there. What a joy to see him! A scarf covered the signs left by his unexpected brain surgery just five weeks earlier. At thirty-two, Eric was much too young to have a cancerous brain tumor.

Then I noticed that he was scheduled to give his testimony. As the worship singing ended, Eric went to the podium and with tears choked back, he told of finding out the Saturday before Easter that he needed surgery the following day. There was no promise that he would make it.

As Eric prepared for what was possibly his final day on earth, he thought of the members of his family who did not know the Lord. He called each one and asked if there was any unfinished business—any wrongs he had not made right. He wept as he explained how just one year earlier he had restored his relationship with his father after fifteen years of bitterness.

Eighty percent of the cancerous tumor was removed, but Eric's future remains uncertain. Chemotherapy and other forms of treatment work to fight the remaining tumor. He had been a notable runner in earlier years, and an article about him in the Los Angeles *Times* led many people who had known him over the years to contact him.

What touched my heart the most about Eric's testimony was his unusual prayer request. He did not ask to be healed; he asked that he would be attuned to the mission, goals, and tasks God had for him before he leaves this earth. His prayer focused on his desire to be an effective witness for Christ in the time he has left. He asked that God would enhance his people skills so that in his day-to-day relationships with those who need Christ he would not be abrasive or insensitive.

As tears rolled down my cheeks, I wondered what I would have said in his situation. Often I find that my day becomes so filled with business that I forget that it could be my final day, week, month, or year to serve Him.

What am I doing with my time? How is my light shining forth? What business goals have not been accomplished? Whom have I touched that knows Christ as his or her personal Savior as a result of my being faithful to God's leading?

Max Lucado says, "You'll be home soon. You may not have noticed it, but you are closer than ever before. Each moment is a step taken. Each breath is a page turned. Each day is a mile marked, a mountain climbed. Before you know it, your appointed arrival time will come: you'll descend the ramp and enter the city."

The psalmist wrote, "Teach us to number our days and recognize how few they are; help us to spend them as we should" (Psalm 90:12, TLB*).

Are we prepared for the unexpected? We need to keep our slate clean. We need to keep dealing with our daily sins of wronging family, friends, or colleagues.

Eric, you continue to be a light to all of us. Your love for the Lord continues to shine. Thank you for challenging us to live our lives so that each moment is measured by God's purpose for our lives.

.

*The Living Bible.

Perspective from a Cemetery

Annie, a dear friend of mine, died recently. She was buried on a high hill overlooking Southern California. Standing there, surrounded by seemingly endless rows of grave markers, you get a different perspective on life, and death. From that vantage point the houses and cars and other material things that seem so precious to us appear small and insignificant.

As we stood around the casket, no one thought about Annie's Mercedes or her beautiful home or jewelry or clothes. We remembered her strong faith, how she wrestled with life and death through her months of suffering and uncertainty. Even in death she was victorious.

We remembered simple acts of kindness. How she welcomed a Vietnamese refugee family into her home. How she was a second mom to neighborhood children. How she shared the joys and wiped away the tears of those in grief.

Annie loved people, so she wanted her memorial service to present the gospel message simply and clearly. She wanted all of her friends to know the way to join her in heaven.

Periodically we need to check the view from the graveyard. It helps us to realize that most of the stuff that fills our minds and causes us stress won't be of any significance a million years from now. A quaint little plaque that my aunt gave me says it well: "Only one life, 'twill soon be past, only what's done for Christ will last."

Peter Drucker had a similar thought when he spoke at a conference. "It's necessary for leadership above all to choose important goals. There should only be a few of them. You should strip away the less important and concentrate your efforts on the few, most important things. The good is the enemy of the best."

If you lose sight of where you are going, your organization is doomed ultimately to failure, no matter how well oiled and financed the machinery. Without a deep commitment to vision, triviality will ultimately triumph.

Like everything important, setting goals does not happen easily or automatically. It requires concentrated and deliberate effort. It is unlikely to happen during the heat of the daily battle.

Goal setting must be planned. Put it on your Daytimer. Close the door, hold your calls, and spend a couple of hours thinking about where the organization is going. Take the long view. If you were to eliminate certain activities, what difference would it make a million years from now? Are we putting our attention to the things God really cares about? Are we letting our hearts be broken with the things that break the heart of God? Or are we just building wood, hay, and stubble—stuff that will go up in flames when this world comes to an end.

Thanks, Annie, for a life of significance. Even in death you gave me the opportunity to focus on priorities. Lord God, help me to spend my time on the eternally significant. Amen.

Personnel—
Employment

Human Resources—
Our Most Valued Gifts

When a management team works together in harmony, humming the same tune and beating the same drum, the whole operation functions well. Isn't it great when everything clicks and everyone shares the same goals and aspirations? Peter Drucker encourages us to remember that all of our human resource staff are volunteers—some paid and some unpaid. They may not be with us forever, but for the time they are part of the organization team we have a responsibility to give them our all in helping them to become leaders for tomorrow.

It is important for us to recognize our responsibility to those individuals. Are we using them to their full potential? Are we paying them what they are worth? Are we wasting our resources on unnecessary expenditures while depriving personnel of a decent living? Have we made employment agreements without fulfilling them? Have we promised to lighten the load but allowed months to pass with no change? Unfulfilled promises negatively reflect not only on key leaders but on the board of directors and the entire organization.

Employees need to be used to their fullest potential. Sometimes we become threatened when an employee excels beyond what we expected. But we need to rejoice in others' accomplishments and continue to challenge them with stimulating projects.

We often find that individuals who are given menial tasks at work are functioning in major leadership roles in their church or community. Such was the case of my banker friend Raymond. While playing golf with a pastor from a neighboring church, he heard eloquent stories of a leader in their church who was in charge of everything. Most of the major church functions were under her volunteer leadership. Raymond said, "She sounds like someone I should hire." When he heard her name, he was speechless. The pastor had been talking about his secretary. Her gifts had gone untapped at work because Raymond had failed to recognize her abilities.

Using testing programs well suited to your organization will help you find talents and interests unique to each employee. It allows for maximum effectiveness for both paid and unpaid employees.

Delegating tasks and authority encourages growth in the whole team. It will also free the leadership team to do their tasks better.

One way to help develop tomorrow's leadership team is to provide adequate continuing education for your staff. This has double benefit. You not only increase their effectiveness, but you also give a strong signal that they are important to you and to the organization. It is a wonderful way to show your appreciation, faith, and trust in personnel and in their continued development.

Integrity with our human resources calls for discipline. It is a daily decision we must make—with God's help. As we look at the potential of those surrounding us, we can remember what Paul says in 2 Corinthians 3:18: "And we, who with unveiled faces all reflect the Lord's glory, are being transformed into his likeness with ever-increasing glory, which comes from the Lord, who is the Spirit."

By His power, we can be known as men and women of integrity by all whose lives we touch. As we focus on the Lord, we will take our directions from Him as He produces His glory in us.

Conflict in the Workplace

No one likes conflict, yet we all face it from time to time. We need to admit that conflict can be a growing and maturing experience and can draw us closer to a person or group after we have struggled through those difficult communication ordeals.

E. M. Houtz, in *Desk Top Devotion*, states it well: "Often, when communication breaks down, it's because we have let it. The result is misunderstanding, and the result of misunderstanding is likely to be a strained or damaged relationship." She further states, "A relationship damaged by conflict and strained by tension can be a real hindrance in the workplace."[1] The sooner we can get to the bottom of conflict and open the lines of communication, the more productive and happier we will be.

I could tell my colleagues were acting strange. You could cut the air with a knife. It was obvious that the two were no longer communicating, and it was beginning to affect everyone. After talking with each one separately, it appeared that there were two completely different stories. We all agreed that the three of us needed to talk. So hard, yet so rewarding. Each was able to express his or her feelings, and both realized that they had misunderstood one another and contributed to the conflict.

Here are some suggestions to follow when faced with conflict:

1. *Be alert.* Don't expect your employees to automatically come to you when they have a complaint. Many times they are afraid of reprisal. Keep ahead of the game by looking for signs of strained relationships.

2. *Recognize warning signs.* If normally happy employees avoid eye contact with you it might be a sign of trouble. If absenteeism or tardiness increases, perhaps a difficult situation has developed. If an employee spends more time alone than usual, a strained relationship may be the reason.

3. *Make trips to the coffee station.* Often the organization grapevine is healthiest at the coffee pot as people are more apt to share the latest news there. This area can often be the best source for "inside information."

4. *Head into the problem at an early stage.* Ignoring it won't cause it to go away. In fact, ignoring difficulties can cause them to escalate and spread to other departments, causing further problems. By heading into the problem early, the situation won't get blown out of proportion and cause an unnecessary explosion.

5. *Collect all the facts.* Make sure that you listen with an open mind. There are always two sides to every story. Make sure the facts are accurate by checking them out and drawing conclusions only after you have heard both sides and verified the information.

6. *Create a climate for healthy confrontation.* Deal with the conflict in a comfortable location where privacy will be guaranteed and where the meeting can have positive resolution. Ask whether emotions are too high to confront at the moment. The state of mind of all parties is important.

7. *Ask questions—don't make accusations.* That will allow for a more open communication between the individuals and diffuse defensiveness. Ask questions that will draw out feelings rather than yes/no answers.

8. *Keep your promise.* If you are part of the solution, and changes need to be made to rectify the situation, make sure you review any promises you have made at the conclusion of the meeting and that you follow through. The

situation could be magnified if further failure occurs because of broken promises.

9. *Check and recheck*. Make sure you not only fulfill your commitments but also have a periodic check-up to ensure that the situation has been taken care of and the employee is happy.

10. *Commit the matter to prayer*. Where we are unable to find solutions, we have the mighty power of God to intervene and bring about reconciliation and healing.

11. *Have a win-win approach*. Knowing that both sides will have rights and both sides will have wrongs, find the points of commonalities. Everyone needs to be heard and to know that some of their concerns were addressed and changes were made.

12. *Forgive and forget*. Don't hold a grudge. Let the issue be history. Bury it at the cross.

Our Savior models the answers perfectly. He didn't just preach it. He cared, He listened, He served, He reached out, He supported, He affirmed and encouraged. He stays in tune and is always there whether we think we need Him or not.

Philippians 3:13-14 says, "Realize that you are not perfect yet, but one thing I do: Forgetting what is behind and straining toward what is ahead, I press on toward the goal to win the prize for which God has called me heavenward in Christ Jesus." Psalm 103:12 says, "As far as the east is from the west, so far has he removed our transgressions from us." Isn't it wonderful that the Lord forgives and forgets? Should that not be our example as we deal with those around us?

As leaders we need to be models. We may not always agree with every idea that comes along, but we should affirm the creative work and the originator.

Conflict kept in balance can be healthy. It gives us the privilege of demonstrating our willingness to grow, and it allows us the opportunity to show God's mercy and grace by having a loving and open attitude toward others.

Are You Dressing for Success?

A manager of a Christian organization talked to me some months ago about an interview he'd had with a woman seeking a position in his organization. The interview time had been set, but she called that morning, asking if the time could be changed from 5:00 to 5:30 P.M. so she could go home and change clothes. He was impressed! However, she arrived dressed in jogging clothes and tennis shoes so she could go jogging after the interview. It was such an overwhelming shock to the manager that he could hardly proceed with the interview. Needless to say, she was not hired.

Another vice president of an organization had been looking for a qualified manager to fill a position for more than three months. He interviewed seven people and none seemed to fit. He had one remaining interview and the candidate, based on his resume, appeared to have all the required qualifications. The vice president was ready to make an offer almost sight unseen. But when the man was ushered into his office, the vice president was disappointed before a word was spoken. The gentleman looked as if he had just finished coaching a soccer match.

Again, the interview lasted a short fifteen minutes, and no offer was made. The candidate almost had the job in his hip pocket. All he had to do was to interview fairly well and he would have achieved a critical step in his career.

Professional dress is most appropriate for men and women looking for new jobs in today's economy. Clothing consultants, such as John T. Molloy, have performed numerous surveys on the attitudes and opinions of employers, customers, and bosses regarding the reactions clothes can generate. The bottom line is that clothes can either make or break you in many situations. Proper clothing can give you the overwhelming competitive advantage or sway the pendulum in your favor when all other factors are equal.

We are often sized up as we walk into an office. It has been said that 85 percent of our assumptions are made in the first seven seconds of a meeting. Often it can take years to undo those early impressions.

What is the professional look? According to John Molloy and other authorities, the best guidelines to follow for a woman's professional look are:

- A two-piece, navy blue or charcoal gray skirted suit of wool, linen, or silk—solids or light pinstripe
- Closed neck blouse
- Closed toe shoe with two-inch medium heel
- Simple gold or silver jewelry—not costume
- No nail polish, no perfume, no purse
- Controlled hair style
- Hemline to cover the knee

A few basic clothing guidelines for men are:

- Three-piece suit—basic solid colors of blue, gray, or beige
- Pinstripe or plain fabric
- White shirt (or light pinstripe design)
- Long sleeved, correctly sized shirt
- Repeated pattern, stripe, or solid ties are all acceptable
- Dark, over-the-calf, well fitted socks
- Simple cuff links

Slight adjustments to our wardrobe can make each of us look more successful and better educated. We can increase our chances of becoming a top executive and stand a much greater chance of succeeding. Creating a proper wardrobe doesn't need to be expensive. Many discount stores provide low cost professional clothing. One manager shopped at a secondhand store where he found a $450 suit for $25.

Dana Henrikson, president of Robert S. Blake Associates, says, "Employers are constantly seeking new people to replace dead wood, individuals suffering from burn-out and those who have reached levels of incompetence. The candidate who looks and acts like he or she already has the job will have a much better chance of being offered the position. Image speaks very loudly. It can make the difference between winning or losing. Image is one of choice not chance."

As ambassadors for Christ, we have an exciting task to "offer [our] bodies as living sacrifices, holy and pleasing to God" (Romans 12:1). The psalmist says, "I praise you because I am fearfully and wonderfully made; your works are wonderful" (Psalm 139:14). We are created in His image. The way we present ourselves professionally is many times key to our success.

Begin today practicing the science of wardrobe engineering to draw a favorable response in important situations. Finally, pray that God's love will shine forth in you as you seek His will for your life.

Are You Boring Yourself to Death?

Living a boring existence will not only spoil the quality of your life; it may even shorten its length. According to studies by Columbia University and the National Institute for Psychosocial Factors in Sweden, boredom is a killer. They found that people with tedious jobs are likely to die prematurely. Employees whose work is repetitive and rigidly controlled and who have little or no contribution to decision making are more at risk for health problems than the overworked, overstressed executive. They concluded that a boring job is equivalent to smoking a pack of cigarettes a day.

To combat boredom, Peter Drucker encourages executives to make management changes every two years. That can be accomplished within the organization through promotion, reassignment, a new project challenge, and so on. Change is good! Learning a new task, a new assignment, a new challenge can increase excitement in employees about their involvement in the business.

According to the December 1987 *Psychology Today*, a study found that elderly people are less likely to die immediately preceding their birthdays than afterward. Having something to look forward to seems to provide them a reason to live. When all the recorded suicides in the United States between 1973 and 1979 were examined, it was found that fewer people killed themselves preceding such holidays as Christmas, Thanksgiving, and the Fourth of July. Apparently they were looking forward to the special event.

The Bible has a message that will help put an end to monotony in tedious day-to-day living. Colossians 3:23 says,

51

"Whatever you do, work at it with all your heart, as working for the Lord, not for men." Another verse says, "In everything give thanks" (1 Thessalonians 5:18, NASB*). If we see everything as a means by which God can perform good in our lives, we are not likely to be bored. Some days it can be very difficult to be thankful, but a thankful heart is a mandate for healthy living.

What can you do to bring new excitement to your job? What can bring newness to your life? Take time to think creatively and bring new stimulation to an otherwise boring job.

McDonald's Corporation executives are required to spend two hours each day in creative thinking. That may not be possible in your organization, but two hours per week could make a tremendous change in your life. Calendar your "creating time." It may be your most important appointment of the week.

I find great stimulation through reading a good management book, talking with a colleague, attending a seminar, studying other organizations to see how they function, and improving my leadership skills. Exercise your creativity to stamp out boredom in your life.

New American Standard Bible.

In Search of Good Board Members

An important aspect of any organization is a board of directors that is well informed and is fulfilling its responsibilities. That doesn't happen overnight. Specific guidelines and procedures need to be in place to ensure that a board is functioning with accountability and integrity.

The Preparation Process

Do your homework. Know what you want before you start looking for candidates. You will need to begin by:

- Determining the ideal board size for your organization
- Determining the representation you desire (geographic, gender, race, church affiliation, professional field, giving history, organization involvement, and so on)
- Preparing an information sheet that will include your expectations of the candidate, such as number of meetings to attend, length of term, roles and responsibilities, financial commitment, and so on
- Collecting data on nominees such as an application form, bio, picture, and other data that can be presented to other members of the board/nominating committee
- Preparing a packet of information on your organization that will help the prospective member understand your vision, including minutes, articles of incorporation, bylaws, brochures, list of expectations, meeting dates, job description, and so on

The Selection Process

Now that your organization's goals and objectives have been incorporated into your board member needs list, you can begin to look for the ideal candidate. Your list needs to be more than names of good friends or wealthy people who can support the organization. David Allan Hubbard of Fuller Theological Seminary stresses the importance of looking for individuals with the three "W's": Work, Wealth, and Wisdom. You may want an individual who has all three, or maybe just one or two of those attributes.

In making your choice:

- Keep alert by making formal and informal contacts to evaluate potential board candidates at company functions.
- Seek recommendations from a variety of sources.
- Paint an honest picture for the candidate, including any financial struggles, legal problems, and so on.
- Communicate thoroughly with the candidate as to why you think he or she could make a valuable contribution to the organization.
- Have a training period so that new board members are fully aware of the organization's goals, visions, and key issues.

Keeping Good Board Members

Volunteer board members don't like to have their time wasted. Be prepared for the meetings. Send materials out well in advance so that members can be prepared and the meeting can move efficiently.

Encourage the board to be team players who can contribute to the purpose of the organization without competing to be stars. According to Frederick T. Spahr, executive director of the American Speech-Language-Hearing Association of Rockville, Maryland, the prospective board member should be a futuristic thinker. He further suggests that attitude is more important than background, expertise, organizational acumen, educational attainment, or anything else.

The attitudes that lead to success in a volunteer board member are based on an awareness of the importance of co-operation and the need to set goals for the organization.

Encourage board members to grow together in harmony by making fellowship and prayer a vital part of your time together. A measure of personal harmony is essential for any group to achieve its goals. Games and personality clashes obscure issues and can damage relationships among board members and within the organization.

Some years ago I served on a board where one of the members had a tremendous ability to work comfortably within conflict situations. He always rose as mediator, having the ability to see both sides of the picture and suggest comfortable resolution between both sides. He was respected by both camps. His calm, level-headed attitude helped board members reach solutions to problems.

A valuable board member keeps an open mind and listens to all sides of an issue. Flexibility is valuable as many diverse thoughts and ideas are shared. Show respect and tolerance for individual interest and personal styles.

Allow all the members to participate and add their comments on relevant issues. Discussions can be greatly enhanced if the chairperson of the board is aware of the dynamics of interaction and makes an effort to call on those who find it harder to get into the discussion.

Members representing a specific segment must recognize that their role is to look at the big picture and recognize that their constituency is the entire membership—not just one geographical area or discipline.

One of the most valuable additions to the Christian Management Association board and committee agendas has been a "brainstorm session"—a time when each board or committee member contributes ideas, dreams, goals, and aspirations for the association. It is a time to dream and open up new areas and ideas for consideration with no financial or other barriers. The ground rules are clear—no one can evaluate the idea as good or bad. No judgments are made as to the financial implications, time, or staff constraints. The statement "It can't be done" is not allowed. A shotgun, rapid-fire approach is the method of this session.

The ideas are then studied, evaluated, and researched by the committees or staff to determine budget constraints and to fit them into the long-range plans for the association.

It is an honor to serve as a board member. Sometimes, however, it may be necessary to recognize when it is not a good time for you to serve. Your wholehearted commitment might not be possible without tremendous cost to your job or family relationships. "But everything should be done in a fitting and orderly way" (1 Corinthians 14:40).

It's Not in My Job Description

You have probably heard employees question their job assignments from time to time—or maybe you have questioned some yourself. When was the last time you read your job description? Do you even have one? When accountability time comes, do you discover that the buck stops with you because none of your subordinates were ever assigned the task? Or, do you discover that the details were yours to carry out, and because you had not reviewed your job description in a long time, you had forgotten about it?

You may know of colleagues who have been "dismissed" or "booted" out the door, utterly confused as to why their services were no longer required. In checking further they found that specific tasks were required of them, but they had never been explained or put into their job description. Worse yet, they thought they were doing an excellent job based on the feedback they had been receiving.

I received a call from a pastor who was concerned about his dismissal of his secretary. She seemed upset and claimed that she was totally unaware that she had not been doing a good job. In fact, she had been receiving numerous compliments from the pastor. The problem was that he had tried to be an encourager, telling her what a great job she was doing, but he had forgotten that the other part of being a manager was to tell his secretary clearly when she was not doing well. He not only needed to spell out what she could do to change but what the consequences would be if she didn't. He had expected her to progress faster than she had, yet he hadn't provided the training she needed to learn the job.

Responsibilities change over time, and perhaps unbeknown to you, so has your job description. Job descriptions are often used as a gauge to review performances, salary increases, promotions. They are sometimes created at the last minute to use in recruiting and never carefully evaluated or updated after the position is filled.

How can you help? If you are working for an organization that does not use a written job description, you are constantly working under assumptions and your knowledge of what is expected of you is unclear.

Maybe it's time to shape up your own area. Begin by writing a job description that best describes your current position. Include an introductory section of general items, a section indicating to whom the position reports, a section on duties and responsibilities, and a final section on standards that are important to the position or the organization.

At your annual review, bring out your job description, and use it as a part of your discussion time. Point out areas where you have gone above and beyond what was expected of you. Your position may have grown and expanded beyond anyone's original intentions. A job description will be a valuable gauge in pointing out areas of growth—and hence a more solid justification for the next salary increase.

You also need to consider updating your job description each year. Employees can use their job description to their own advantage by not only fulfilling the requirements but by influencing its development. Your boss will have a greater comprehension of what your responsibilities are, and your replacement will not have to suffer through the same "state of confusion" you functioned with.

Begin today! If your job description hasn't been updated, if you don't have one, or if your employees don't have one, maybe it's time to update or start from scratch and write one.

The Commitment to Teamwork

I worked for a church some years ago and saw Rose dutifully making three-by-five-inch cards of all of the hundreds of church members. When I asked what she was doing and why, she said, "Pastor asked me to do it, and I don't know why." At that point, she had worked for several weeks on the project. After further research, I discovered that the pastor who asked her to do it did not know that our new office technology allowed us to accomplish the task in a fraction of the time. The team was not functioning properly. The left hand didn't know what the right hand was doing, and it was a costly and discouraging realization to Rose.

For some, being a team player doesn't come naturally, so it needs to be demonstrated from the top. We can forget that the end result has been an effort of many individuals working together. The visionary is important to get the ideas out on the table. The organizer keeps the project moving along to meet the targeted due date. The researcher is valuable in collecting accurate data so that decisions can be made based on facts. The typist is important in putting together an accurate and neat report. The mail clerk is necessary to getting the data out the door to the right destination. If a team works hard to complete the project and one member fails to act with excellence and a commitment to detail, the whole project fails.

I received a package in June that had been mailed the December before. The mailing department had put the package on the shelf "temporarily," and it was discovered six months later. One member of the team had slipped up. Slip-ups like that are costly to an organization and guarantee poor customer service relations.

In his book *The Quest for Character*, Chuck Swindoll states that an important ingredient in effective teamwork is love. "Nothing . . . absolutely nothing pulls a team closer together or strengthens the lines of loyalty more than love. It breaks down internal competition. It silences gossip. It builds morale. It promotes feelings that say, 'I belong' and 'Who cares who gets the credit?' and 'I must do my very best' and 'You can trust me because I trust you.'"[2]

U.S. Army General Norman Schwarzkopf was a great example of a leader committed to teamwork in the Gulf War. He never missed a chance to credit his people for their roles in the victory. Each member of the team was made to feel important and part of the big picture.

When the whole team works together and is successful with their efforts, the praise and credit needs to be shared by all. Satisfaction comes when everyone's efforts are recognized.

Personnel— Motivation

Cheerleading—
A Transferable Concept?

We were losing the most crucial game of the season. I was seventeen, a cheerleader for my tiny, rural Minnesota high school. Our guys were discouraged. It looked as if there was no hope (and nothing seems more important than a football game when you're seventeen, remember?). Then we got a good cheer going, and somehow our exhausted guys found the extra ounce of energy that they needed to turn the game around.

The team needed encouragement. They needed to be stretched for success, and they needed the support of the student body to pull them together to reach for the goal of winning.

Cheerleading makes a difference in high school football games, and I think it makes a difference in life as well. Leaders have a challenge to find the right people, place them where they can perform to their fullest potential, and cheer them on.

If we let our employees know that they are a vital part of the team, they will not only feel great about their jobs personally, but they will convey that excitement to those they interact with throughout the day.

Most of us need to be motivated to stretch. It's not something that comes naturally. We need to learn how to stretch ourselves, but we also need to know how to motivate others to reach their potential.

The number one cause of job stress isn't overwork. It's feeling unvalued. It is important that our associates know they are doing their jobs well. We are all held accountable for what we do with the talents we have been given. Many studies show that those who believe their abilities are being challenged and used are enthusiastic and produce results. Unchallenging jobs result in nonproductivity and a cynical attitude.

Peter Drucker says, "Each job should be demanding and big and challenge the person to bring out whatever strength they may have." Drucker maintains that most people use only 2 to 5 percent of their capabilities. If that is true, we still have 95 percent of our capabilities to develop and use. By "cheering them on" we can help employees discover and use more of their God-given abilities.

Each of us can get discouraged at times. The best way to pull out of discouragement is to surround yourself with encouragers, with individuals who understand the value of affirmation and who believe in you. Often the best way to find other encouragers is to become one yourself. Discovery always comes in an encouraging environment. Find someone who will help you discover who you are and what you can do. Discovering your gifts from God will start you toward a world of reaching your potential.

Staff Growth and Development from the Start

A strong personnel management program is essential for every organization. We can run more effective programs by following these steps.

- Create current and up-to-date position descriptions for all employees. That provides a format and base for employees to grow and develop. When updates are needed, the employees do it with guidance from their supervisor.

- Write a carefully tailored employee handbook, covering policies, standards, compensation, benefits, leaves, and any legal statements necessary to maintain current requirements. Require each employee to sign and return a form indicating that he or she has read and understands it.

- Provide a procedures manual for consistent work flow. Update it regularly so that it can be used as a valuable resource for new employees as they work through the learning process.

- Provide a packet of materials such as brochures, schedule of events, mission and purpose statements, list of board members and important constituents, and any materials that adequately describe the organization and its programs.

- Schedule an orientation and training program for new employees, using staff members as resources. Include a meeting with appropriate department heads and program directors, allowing them to explain their department programs for ten to fifteen minutes. Include the little things, such as a time to become acquainted with office machines and frequently used vendors, such as supply and mail centers.

- Provide a list of "frequently asked questions" and answers.
- Clearly spell out the goals and expectations for the next quarter, and help staff prepare annual goals.
- Schedule frequent appraisal sessions to let staff know how they are doing and to make any necessary course corrections.
- Communicate employees' opportunities for advancement and what performance is expected to reach new levels.
- Inform new employees of the procedure for airing grievances so that when they have a concern they will know where to turn.
- Schedule weekly staff meetings to help new employees get the "big picture" quickly as various team members talk about their projects.
- Communicate changes to the entire team on an ongoing basis. That will avoid embarrassment due to lack of knowledge.

Because of hectic schedules recently, I found that I had not done an adequate job of training a new employee. She became discouraged and was ready to resign. When I realized that I was the cause of her discouragement, I quickly began a more thorough job of training to restore her confidence.

We need to invest time and attention in new employees. A good training program will help them feel part of the team quickly and will shorten the transition phase as they get up to speed and grow to be effective employees. The payoff is worth the extra time.

How to Train, Motivate, and Keep Your Staff

Leaders need to find the right people and place them in the right places so that they can perform to their fullest potential. That can be an awesome responsibility.

Surveys show that those who are enthusiastic and produce results are those who are being challenged and used. Most people use only a tiny fraction of their ability. The exciting news is that most of their capabilities are still untapped.

The Training Process

Vince Lombardi, one of the greatest football coaches of our time, started each season by going back to the basics. He began by saying, "OK, fellahs, this is a football." One year a wise guy responded, "Hey, coach, not so fast."

The training process is important. *The One Minute Manager*, by Blanchard and Johnson, states, "Most companies spend 50-70% of their money on people's salaries. And yet they spend less than 1% of their budget to train their people. Most companies, in fact, spend more time and money on maintaining their buildings and equipment than they do on maintaining and developing people."[3]

Remember that new people and programs require time to take hold and grow. In most cases, it takes a minimum of six months to a year for an individual to rise to full levels of productivity. Continual feedback during that intense learning time is vital.

Provide the tools they need. They need to be encouraged to professional growth, including professional memberships, reading materials, lectures, conferences, and other activities that will stimulate development and refinement of skills.

Motivation Needs

We all need to be encouraged and praised. I have enjoyed listening to Tommy LaSorda as he explained how he has motivated and built up the Los Angeles Dodgers. He helps them believe they are winners, that they can do it. He goes wild with enthusiasm.

We need to be cheerleaders for our team. They will respond beautifully to praise and affirmation. *The One Minute Manager* encourages us to "Tell people how good you feel about what they did right, and how it helps the organization and the other people who work there." And further, to "tell people what they did right and be specific."[4]

There are many ways to recognize your staff. How you do it is not as important as that it be done.

Retaining Your Staff

The Bureau of National Affairs estimates that employee turnover rates are about 22 percent per year for most companies. Many Christian organizations are guilty of *using* their people instead of *valuing* them. The result is low morale, high turnover, and a high level of disillusionment.

A call came from a woman seeking a place where she could serve. She made this statement: "I have now worked for two different Christian organizations, and it has been such a difficult experience that I simply don't want to work for another Christian organization."

God directs us to practice the "one anothers" in Scripture—loving, encouraging, exhorting, admonishing, and building others up. Ultimately we will have to stand before God when He asks us, "What have you done with my people?"

Vessels of Encouragement

Compliments can ease tensions, mend relationships, and revitalize the spirits, not only of the receiver but also of the giver.

When was the last time you uplifted the people you work with, your family, your friends? If you can't remember, you need to begin now. Look for things to compliment in those around you, yes, even in the difficult person in your office. Once you start to encourage others, you will also begin to see the change in those individuals. As you fill their lives with cheer, their cup will overflow into the lives of others.

I am reminded of the many encouragers in my life—those friends who always seem to hold the rope for me during difficult times, those individuals who drop me notes to say, "You did a great job on that," or, "I really appreciate what you do for me." I am blessed by those who make an effort to show they care and to give that extra boost when the pressures mount, when the concerns seem too heavy to bear.

A few years ago I was looking for something that we could use in our office to say, "Well done." Knowing my desire, a dear friend purchased a bike horn and had it mounted on a piece of wood so we could hang it on the wall. It has become our way of "tooting our own horn" or "tooting someone else's horn" when we conquer a mountain, complete a difficult task, balance the books, finish typing the extra-long report, and so on. Affirming an individual in the presence of others not only helps to build the team spirit but also helps us remember the difficult tasks and pressures of those around us. As one person is uplifted, so is the team.

Sometimes it is easier to point out the errors of others than to point out what is done right. In *The One Minute Manager*, the authors say, "Most managers wait until their people do something exactly right before they praise them. As a result, many people never get to become high performers because their managers concentrate on catching them doing things wrong—that is, anything that falls short of the final desired performance."[5] The one-minute praise works. Give it a try. Remember, praise is public, but reprimand is private.

Pray for those who come to mind. As I listen to friends and colleagues, I often find myself asking if I can pray with them before we hang up. On several occasions the suggestion has come as a surprise to the caller. Yet, as we tune in to people's needs, we can hear their cry—their need for a job or for assistance in their management problem, or whatever their concern might be.

Don't miss the opportunity to ask the Lord's direction in solving that difficult problem or to ask God to give a friend courage and strength. When individuals come to mind throughout the day, I believe it is God's way of reminding us to pray for them. You may be the only one holding the rope for an individual at that time. Perhaps you are the person God has called to support him or her in prayer. Send a note or a personal touch to show that you care.

"Then when he had come and witnessed the grace of God, he rejoiced and began to encourage them all with resolute heart to remain true to the Lord" (Acts 11:23, NASB).

May we be known as encouragement givers and individuals who bring joy to those around us.

Is Appreciation a Thing of the Past?

Recently, I conducted a seminar on office administration, where administrators and secretaries were in attendance. I asked how many secretaries had been remembered by their boss in a tangible way for anything they had done.

I was disappointed to see that several hands did not go up. Some had bosses who were just too busy to take the time to show appreciation for a job well done!

If you are patting yourself on the back because you remember Secretaries' Day, I'd like to ask—what have you done recently? How have you stopped to thank those who pour hours of faithful service into your organization?

I was disappointed in myself recently when a staff person had struggled long hours, worked weekends, stayed late, and diligently worked on his project to the bitter end. When the finished product arrived on my desk, did I praise and thank him for the tremendous job? No, I turned to the front section, saw two lines in the wrong place, and promptly pointed them out. I could have kicked myself when I saw the disappointment in his face. How could I have been so thoughtless? The praise that followed when I realized what I'd done didn't make up for my blunder.

Is showing appreciation a thing of the past? Perhaps you think that your staff receive regular paychecks and that that is thanks enough.

To most people, it is not enough! Job satisfaction is measured not by the "green stuff" that comes on payday but by the "warm fuzzies" that come each day to show your appreciation.

Being conscious of ways that you can regularly and sincerely show appreciation is a beginning. Productivity often increases in direct proportion to the amount of praise and affirmation we show our colleagues.

The church secretary had just received the fifth phone call from a member pointing out that "church" was not spelled "chirch." In her frustration, she hung up the phone, turned to her boss, and asked, "Why hasn't anyone mentioned the thirty-three hundred words I did spell correctly?"

We need to remember a simple six-letter word: thanks.

Here are some suggestions for tangibly expressing appreciation:

- Award the employee of the month or week by placing a trophy on his or her desk. It will be a reminder to fellow colleagues that they have made a significant contribution to the organization as well.
- Send a "Thank You gram" or "Warm Fuzzy gram" to an employee.
- Take an employee out to lunch and tell him how valuable he is and how his attitude and service contribute to the success of the organization.
- Have a special parking space reserved for the employee of the month.
- Give a bouquet of flowers or another appropriate item to your secretary or assistant.
- Try the "ten penny approach," putting ten pennies in one pocket at the beginning of the day. Each time you affirm someone, move a penny into the opposite pocket. Try to have all the pennies moved from one pocket to the other by the end of the day.
- Have an appreciation banquet annually for employees and volunteers, presenting awards and certificates of merit.
- Give a new and challenging assignment to a subordinate to show your faith and trust in his or her skills.
- Give a merit raise to show the value of an individual's skills.
- Surprise someone—get a "cup of cold water" or coffee for your secretary instead of waiting for her to bring it to you.

- As you sign the stack of letters today, tuck a note midway through that says, "Great job! Sure glad you're part of the team."

Statistics show that the second highest stress-related job in the nation is the secretarial position. Help relieve some of the stress today. Be an encourager—a praise hunter rather than an error hunter.

A Kinder and Gentler Day

Is your "To Do" list completed? Is your desk free of clutter? Are you refreshed and filled with the joy that you have completed everything? Are all your projects running on time? Will deadlines be met with no problems?

The answer to most of those questions for many of us is a resounding NO! We have difficult days, disappointment, and discouragement that sometimes threaten to overwhelm us.

Perhaps you still have not found the job that you have been searching and praying for, for months. You have asked many whys, and none of them has been answered. In times like that we especially appreciate the love and concern of friends and family.

When others are hurting it is important to reach out, showing kindness. It helps to hear "We are praying for you," "We hurt when you hurt," "I'm here to hold the rope for you today."

As you begin to focus on the day ahead as a kinder and gentler day, you will begin to see the needs of others around you. As you fill their lives with cheer, it will spill over into many other lives.

Mary is the kind of friend that brings cheer to my life. The sound of her voice can lift my spirits. After a tough day, a short visit with Mary can change a sad heart to a heart of joy. She bubbles with enthusiasm and excitement for life, and it's contagious.

Scripture actually commands us to encourage one another. "Let us encourage one another—and all the more as you see the Day approaching" (Hebrews 10:25). And Hebrews 3:13 says, "Encourage one another daily." It is not only a requirement, but a privilege. When we give words of encouragement or do an uplifting act—send a card or a note of affirmation—we bring positive energy to our colleagues.

David J. Schwartz, a sales consultant and author of *The Magic of Thinking Big*, says, "Practice appreciation, first by offering people who work for you honest, personalized compliments on their achievements. . . . Treating someone as second class never gets you first-class results." He also encourages us to

> develop the habit of calling people by their names, provided you also take care to pronounce them correctly. . . . Our positive attitudes toward ourselves and toward other people matter as much or more than basic competence: Employees will work harder for you, associates will go out of their way to cooperate with you, your boss will do more to help you if you will only make these people feel important and loved.[6]

Schwartz also encourages us to pass good news along rather than taking all the praise and credit or quietly savoring our company's success. "Praise," he says, "can be invested to pay dividends."

Let's give the gift of encouragement and kindness to those around us. Be known for the happiness you will bring today, wherever you go.

Sex Roles

Sexism Is Alive and Sick
in Christian Organizations

Sexism isn't sick in the sense that it's about to die out. I wish that were true. Instead, it's a disease, a blight. And it keeps the Body of Christ from functioning as well as it could and should.

What Is Sexism?

I would define sexism as any unnecessary difference in the way you deal with men and women, though some differences in treatment are dictated by the physical differences between the sexes. Men don't give birth to babies or nurse them. Women are usually shorter and weaker than men. It's silly to ignore those differences but devastating to overplay them.

Sexism is when women are paid less or given less honor than men for work of equal value. I was irritated recently when my church asked all of the pastoral staff (all male) and their families to stand, whereas not any of the secretarial staff or the business manager (all female) was even acknowledged. When women work as hard as the men do for about half of the salary and no recognition, that's sexism.

Sexism is in play when a man is preferred for a job that a woman could do as well. Though more women than men graduate from college these days and women have higher grades on the average, they are still significantly behind in salaries and advancement opportunities. Worse yet, discrimination against women seems to be more prevalent in Christian organizations than in secular. Is that the image Christ would have us present?

Sexual Harassment

The number of cases of sexual harassment found in churches and Christian organizations is shocking. Sexual harassment is any unwanted and inappropriate sexually oriented behavior toward a member of the opposite sex. It could range from a careless remark, "Women are always gossiping," to a blatant demand for sexual favors.

As I travel around the country I am often approached by women asking how to rebuff the sexual advances of their supervisors or co-workers. Every organization should have a well-defined program in place so that individuals can confidentially seek answers about sexual harassment. It must be done with the assurance that it will be kept confidential and not hamper their work relations.

If you think your organization has no problem with sexual harassment, I suggest that you give the female members of your staff a way to confidentially or anonymously report such events and watch the results.

Some years ago I led a weekend management retreat where I encouraged women to sign up for fifteen-minute private discussions with me during their two hours of free time. All eight slots were filled, and six of the eight asked how to handle unwanted sexual advancements from their pastor or boss. One indicated that the pastor was pressing her to go on a date and his wife worked in the church office. Many complainers felt paralyzed with nowhere to turn.

At a different meeting, a pastor revealed that a female parishioner was stalking him and trying to trap him in private settings to "get something going."

Men and women alike need to guard against sexual temptations.

Causes of Sexism

1. *Misapplication of Scripture.* I believe many in church circles misapply Paul's admonitions for order in the church and home to somehow justify inequality for workers in Christian organizations.
2. *History.* We have been reared in a sexist society. The old ways are not necessarily right or just, but it's hard to change.
3. *Women.* Women may actually be as guilty as men. Some women dress more to be "cute" than competent. Provocative dress and behavior seem to invite sexual advances. Women may also settle too easily for low-level jobs or poor pay.
4. *Insensitivity.* Most Christian managers do not deliberately set out to discriminate and are shocked to find that they do.

How to Reduce Sexism in Your Organization

Each cause above suggests an answer. First, we need to think clearly about what the Bible really says about male and female roles and how it applies in today's nonagrarian society. Pastors, seminaries, and Christian colleges, as well as Christian organizations, need to forge ahead on this front.

We need to become more aware of how mistakes in the past have conditioned our thinking in harmful ways. We should not be *indiscriminately* conservative. We should be willing to move away from the errors of the past while preserving the good.

Women need to recognize their part in contributing to sexism. Eleanor Roosevelt said, "You can't make me feel inferior without my complete cooperation."

Finally, we must all become more sensitive to the devastation caused by sexism. More than half of all adults are women, and approximately two-thirds of Christians are women. Women, like men, are gifted for ministry. There are many biblical models for women in ministry, even in leadership positions. There is plenty of work for all of us, so let's find just and equitable ways to work together.

Opening Communication Lines

While attending a conference recently, I was deeply impressed by the two male facilitators who led the mixed group of leaders. Fifty percent of the time when referring to board members, leaders, and so on, they used "she," and 50 percent of the time they said "he." It was a breath of fresh air as I had just returned from a convention where I felt totally bypassed because of the exclusive use of "he" throughout the entire presentation.

Inclusive communication skills are extremely important these days. It takes discipline and a determination to set aside old habits. Many think that when people hear "generic" words such as "mankind" and "he," they respond inclusively, instinctively understanding that the terms apply to both sexes. After studying the issue, however, Myra Sadker, author of *The Communications Gender Gap*, by the Mid-Atlantic Center for Sex Equality, found that such an assumption is incorrect. She further found that even though it is assumed that women talk more than men, actually men talk more than women. According to her research, when a male speaks he is listened to more carefully than a female speaker, even if an identical presentation is made.

As the number of women in leadership increases, it is important that gender assumptions be challenged. Stereotypes can cut off communication and cause hurt feelings.

Over the years I have collected gender stereotype assumptions:

- Women are expected to be more cheery than men.
- Men are expected to be tough and not cry.
- The higher pay should go to the man.
- Women, not men, should miss work to care for sick children.
- Women are better communicators.
- Men have more ego problems.
- Women are better academically.

The problem with functioning as if assumptions were facts is that people simply don't fit into boxes. We are all created uniquely and have characteristics that break the standard mold. My husband is tough but cries easily and often. It takes a lot to bring me to tears, yet I am tender.

I was amused one day when I heard a businessman say that one of his male directors was "really good with details." Yet, the same man said his female director was "picky." Perhaps he should have put more thought into his assessments. Clearly both were detail people, and both were picky. One, however, was given the negative stigma.

We all have the right to be listened to and taken seriously, the right to be treated with respect, the right to express our feelings and opinions, and the right to get paid fairly for what we do.

Dealing with Sexual Harassment
in the Christian Workplace

In the days after the allegations against Supreme Court nominee Clarence Thomas by law professor Anita Hill became public, the workplace buzzed with questions about sexual harassment. If we thought it didn't happen among Christians, we have proof that we were wrong. If we think it doesn't happen in the safety of the Christian office environment, we are wrong again. It does!

We must be familiar with the law so that everyone knows exactly what sexual harassment is. Many don't understand the law, and they are worried.

What is sexual harassment? It is unwelcome sexual advances, requests for sexual favors, or verbal or physical conduct of a sexual nature (such as name calling, suggestive comments, or lewd talk) when any one of the following three factors is present:

1. Submission to that conduct is made either explicitly or implicitly a term or condition of the individual's employment.
2. Submission to or rejection of a request for sexual favor becomes a basis for a decision concerning an individual's employment.
3. The conduct is unreasonably interfering with the individual's work performance or creates an intimidating, hostile, or offensive work environment.

As was stated throughout the Thomas-Hill hearings, 180 days is the statute of limitations. Some state laws run from 60 days to three years. One area that is not accepted across the board by the courts is bystander harassment— where an individual witnesses someone else being harassed. In any case, the company should build an environment where sexual harassment is not tolerated in any form.

Consulting with experts is critically important. Where policies don't exist—create them. Employers need to have a clear, comprehensive policy and procedure within the workplace so that employees and supervisors have a clear understanding of "what happens now." The policy statement needs to tell everyone that sexual harassment is not tolerated and anyone who engages in it is subject to discipline, including discharge.

Unlike the Clarence Thomas hearings, complete confidentiality must be guaranteed. Victims must find a safe way to say, "Stop, I don't like or appreciate the way you are treating me. It is unwelcome attention, and if it doesn't stop, you will be breaking the law." Employees need to know where they can turn, that they will be heard, that the allegations will be presented to the harasser, and that the problem will be corrected.

A warning and clear message to the harasser, along with steps that need to take place to correct the problem, should be presented verbally and in writing.

The federal law doesn't excuse lack of knowledge. It is management's responsibility to know the law, enforce it, and provide a safe place where complaints can be heard and acted upon. If management ignores the issue, they are subjecting themselves and their organization to legal liability if an individual files a charge.

Sexual harassment may not necessarily come from colleagues. Management is also liable for an outside salesperson or vendor who comes into your workplace on a regular basis. Supervisors must be prepared and keep a watchful eye and ear.

In these days of high sensitivity regarding this issue, it would be well advised to distribute your written policy to all employees and discuss any areas of the law that may need further clarification in a staff meeting.

Studies show that 15 percent of the sexual harassment cases reported are reported by men who have experienced sexual harassment from women. Women are not above abusing their power.

According to Cathie Cowie, CEO of Alston-Kline, a human resource consulting firm in Edmonds, Washington, "An organization that has a significant representation of women in senior management positions shows that the organization promotes, respects, and encourages growth for women." She further says, "It also means men will be less likely to engage in harassment because having female peers will inhibit them. The best deterrent to harassment in the workplace is a working atmosphere that says all are equal."

Don't be afraid to address the issue. It is never an easy subject, but it is critical to the process of a "sexual harassment free environment" in the company.

Women in a Challenging Role

Would you prefer to work for a man or a woman? Does it matter? The majority of men and women still prefer to work for men, probably because that is what we have been used to. Today, however, the presence of women in management is growing.

Men generally feel more comfortable when they have the power because they've had that role since they were old enough to play in the sandbox. Boys were told, "Big boys don't cry." They were taught to be strong and powerful. Girls, on the other hand, received affirmation for being "Daddy's little girl."

I am grateful for my heritage. I grew up in a family where there was a strong mother with a professional career before marriage. My mother's seven sisters were also career women, so my role models were rather atypical. My parents' examples taught me to be a hard worker, a leader, self-sufficient, dependable, and strong. There was no tolerance for family members who were not willing to be part of the farm team—even when it meant I was on the tractor doing typically male tasks.

For many women, being in a position of power is new, and they may have a tendency to misuse that power. Women need to receive power with gentleness and remember that God has called us all to be servant leaders. Leaders are really at the bottom supporting the whole team.

Women don't need to act like men to be successful. They should be encouraged to relax and use the special and unique gifts God has given them.

Men and women alike agree that female managers bring sensitivity to the job. Historically sensitivity has not been an attribute found in the top ten list of management traits. Today, however, it is a valued trait. Women often have more empathy for people than men do, and they bring added sensitivity to the management table.

When a woman prepares for a leadership role, here are some important things to remember:

- Do what needs to be done without grumbling.
- Do your job well.
- Believe in yourself.
- Dress appropriate to the position you seek to attain.
- Find your own network of competent men and women mentors to assist your growth.
- Be trustworthy and honest.
- Don't let your emotions get out of control (there isn't much room for failure).
- Learn to evaluate and receive criticism without feeling personally attacked.
- Volunteer for projects that will demonstrate your leadership.
- Know your strengths and weaknesses, and use your giftedness.
- Pray for God's leading and direction for your life, and trust Him.

Amelia Earhart said, "Some of us have great runways already built for us, and if you have one, just take off. But if you don't have one, it's your job to grab the shovel."

Moving into leadership positions may not be easy for women, but life never is easy. It is challenging and exciting to work hard and watch as the Lord begins to place you in significant leadership positions for His glory.

Ethics

Let Your Fingers Do the Talking

A minister was being shown through a textile mill where one of his parishioners worked. Mentioning the employee to the foreman, the pastor said, "I suppose John is one of your best workers."

The foreman responded, "No, I'm sorry to say he isn't. The trouble with John is that he stands around talking about his religion when he ought to be tending to his loom. He hasn't learned yet that while he is on the job his religion ought to come out his fingers and not his mouth."

A wise observation. Honest labor can be a strong testimony. When we rob our employer through half-hearted attention to our jobs, our testimony suffers.

These days it is an understatement to say that Christians are being watched. Integrity—the bringing together of words and actions—is often missing, unfortunately. The Christian and secular media flood us with *words*. We crave *action*—loving, kind, just, sacrificial action to give meaning to the words.

You have heard it said, "Our actions speak so loudly that the world can't hear what we say." That doesn't put it strongly enough. I think our actions are often so crummy that they *ridicule* what we say.

Goof-off Christians aren't just a problem in the secular world, either. I once had an employee I'll call Jim. He continually found time to visit with other workers though he had stacks of work to do.

When I asked him why he wasted so much time and interrupted other people's work, his answer almost sounded spiritual. He said, "Well, I have to find out what their needs are so I can witness to them or try to help solve their problems."

I suggested that the witnessing could be done during the evening hours. He shot back, "Oh, no, I simply don't have time at night—I am much too busy with my family." Amazing! He couldn't see the problem of *stealing* time from his employer, but he wasn't willing to give up his own time.

Christian organizations may, in fact, suffer more from that problem than secular companies. We are, after all, caring and giving people. We don't like to come down hard on our employees. But if we let our workers get by with shoddy work practices, we are not being good stewards. When we tolerate dishonesty, our organization is not modeling what the Master intended.

What to do about it? Here are some ideas.

- Make sure your employees know what you expect. Many people, especially those new to the work force, really don't know what is expected. Be specific. For example, you might want to establish that no more than five minutes per hour should be spent on personal business (not counting coffee breaks and lunch).

- Make sure you have some way of monitoring productivity. If you can't closely observe your people, you might have them fill out a log sheet listing what they are doing in each six-minute period.

- Let them know that you care about productivity. Reward those who produce. If you can't find a way to increase the productivity of lazy workers, show them the door.

- Set an example. If you habitually come in at ten, leave at three, and take a two-hour lunch break, you aren't setting a very good example! Who are *you* accountable to?

Let's realize that time is our most valuable resource. Leaders are responsible for how time is used. Don't let it be stolen or wasted. Let's take stewardship seriously.

Faithfulness in Little

All too often in our busy days, we are faced with ethical decisions that seem to be of no real consequences. It is easy to compromise in tiny ways, but when we do, we begin the "slippery slope" that leads to major moral failure.

There are many ways we can compromise our walk with the Lord each day. Do we take stamps or supplies that don't belong to us? Do we steal time or waste time that we are being paid for? When we travel, do we fudge on our expense report? Is our mileage reporting accurate? Do we take liberties with reimbursements that we expect from the ministry?

A leader of a ministry told me recently that one of his directors put in an expense receipt for $150 of dry cleaning. He was asked to justify the charge. The explanation was that he had been traveling and his suits needed cleaning and he thought the ministry should clean them. How could that possibly be justified? Wouldn't the entire ministry team feel the freedom to hold off on their cleaning until they 'went on the road,' so the ministry would foot the bill? And a person working at the home office would have had the same need for cleaning. Such decisions do not fall within the boundaries of integrity.

A frustrated employee asked me what was ethical for reimbursed expenses for her boss. She said, "He and his family went on a four-week vacation, spending three days of the time at a conference where he spoke. The rest of the month was spent touring the country. He turned in all of the travel, hotel, and meal costs for reimbursement." She struggled with the integrity of this action. I was horrified by the example being set. The CEO's conscience had obviously been dulled to the point that he apparently didn't think he was using ministry money unjustly.

Do we dull our consciences by making small compromising decisions each day? Do such choices affect our ability to be used effectively by God? Do we want to risk the blessing of the Lord on our lives or on our ministry?

Keep your conscience clear! If in doubt, don't. Don't squelch the Spirit of God. Ask your colleagues, supervisor, or board member for their feedback. One way to test whether you are making a sound decision is to ask yourself, How will I feel if someone finds out? If it would cause embarrassment, you are functioning in a compromising way.

Here are some guidelines to help protect you from temptation:

- Make sure your ministry has clear policies and guidelines.
- If there are no policies, write them.
- If policies are unclear, clarify them.
- Communicate clearly to the entire team what are acceptable and unacceptable guidelines of integrity.
- Make yourself accountable to someone for all your expenditures.
- Don't assume that everyone functions within the guidelines. Have systems to check and recheck the team's integrity.
- Pray that the Lord will quicken our spirits to the temptations of the evil one and lead us to resist his lures.

Matthew 25:23 says, "Well done, good and faithful servant! You have been faithful with a few things; I will put you in charge of many things." Joseph was tempted, but he remained faithful to his master and to God. He did not fail. Because he could consistently be trusted, Pharaoh put him in charge. He was given the highest position he could occupy in an alien land.

Keeping Your Word

Do you work with people you can trust? If they say, "I'll call you at 10:00 A.M." will your phone ring at 10:00 because they are men and women of their word?

I was working with a company that wanted to provide insurance for our organization. We were promised the world. Days passed with no word from them. We called our representative, who said, "I was just picking up the phone to call you." We asked for the information he had promised, but it was unavailable. He promised, "I'll have it for you by tomorrow at 9:00 A.M." The appointed time came and went—and days passed again with no word. Once again we called, and he said, "I was just picking up the phone to call you." We realized that was the last call we would make to that gentleman. His word meant nothing.

The Billy Graham organization signed a contract with the City of Albany, New York, for an eight-day crusade. Mr. Graham was unexpectedly hospitalized, and the crusade had to be called off. Under normal contracts, penalties of up to 75 percent of the value of the conference would have been assessed. According to Carol McCullough, director of sales and marketing for the Desmond Americana hotel, "The crusade people were forthright about sharing the costs involved. But since they re-booked for July and because they are so professional in dealing with our hotel, and the city as well, the hotel and the Knickerbocker arena waived any penalty charges." The Graham organization didn't risk their word of honor. They are to be commended for their step of faithfulness and integrity. They didn't risk their word of honor nor that of the

Christian community in general. Their example stands in stark contrast to those of whom it is said, "I won't do business with those Christians any more because they simply don't keep their word."

If you want to persuade people to trust in you, these guidelines might help:

- Never make a promise you can't fulfill.
- Never make a decision you can't support.
- Don't threaten. Never issue an order you can't enforce.
- Don't exaggerate. Be accurate and truthful in your statements.
- When you make a commitment, calendar the promise as if it is a luncheon appointment.
- If it becomes impossible for you to fulfill your commitment, call or have someone call on your behalf to explain the change.
- Make a decision to change if it's needed.
- Be quick to admit when you are wrong and ask for forgiveness.

Unnecessary disappointments arise when we carelessly agree that we will do something and then forget. Trust is damaged or even destroyed. Those who are faithful have found a way to make sure that when they make a promise they mark it down and fulfill it. They work hard to be men and women of their word. God has called us to be faithful in word and deed.

Faithful and Trustworthy

While watching football in mid-September, I heard a commentator discussing the character of Paul "Bear" Bryant. "His word was all that was necessary—you could take it to the bank—he would fulfill his promise!" Could that be said of you and me?

Would that trust in Christian organizations was so high and the degree of confidence so strong that this statement could be made: "Moreover, they did not require an accounting from the men into whose hand they gave money to pay to those who did the work, for they dealt faithfully" (2 Kings 12:15, NASB).

If we are known for constant tardiness, chronic absences, or our failure to carry out responsibilities, how can anyone feel comfortable doing business with us? The question is no longer, "Whom can I trust?" but rather, "Can I trust anyone?"

Matthew 25:23 says, "You have been faithful with a few things; I will put you in charge of many things." If we are unfaithful in the small things, does it mean we will be unfaithful in the bigger things?

One of the most difficult things to happen to any of us is to lose our trust in someone or to cause someone else's trust in us to be shaken. When my daughter was five years old, she took a twenty-dollar bill from my purse. When I discovered it in her little purse, I asked her where she got it. She confessed that she had taken it from me. I explained how serious a matter it was and that she should never do it again. She looked quite puzzled and then responded, "Well, it's only a dollar."

As we talked, I explained that it was a twenty-dollar bill but that it didn't matter whether it was a one or a twenty; either way, it was stealing, and my trust in her had been shaken. More than anything else, that got to her. She was upset by the fact that I no longer trusted her. She decided that she wanted to work hard to rebuild my trust in her.

Trust is not a gift. It has to be earned.

It is often the little things that cause us to lose our trust in people. It is "forgetting" a promise or considering it unimportant when your word, and that of your organization, is at stake.

Some years ago, when I worked for another company, security arrived in the office asking for one of my colleagues. When she arrived, she was asked to clean out her desk and leave. She had embezzled several thousand dollars from the company through improper refunds that she had cashed later. New procedures were quickly instigated, but the damage had been done and with it came a new level of mistrust for everyone. Accountability is an important ingredient in any organization.

U.S. News and World Report stated that workers who steal time on the job cost the American economy $120 billion in wages paid but not earned. That is three times more than the cost of recognized business crimes. In addition, $50 billion is lost in employee theft of materials.[7]

Industry Week reported that, in 1964, 13 percent of American workers stole from their employers. Twenty years later that figure was 30 percent. Additionally, *Communication Briefings* stated that the average employee spends sixty-two hours each year making personal calls on the office phone. Christian organizations aren't exempt from this.

Each of us can make a difference. Our actions speak loudly. The world may not hear a word we are saying—but it is watching our every move. We have a big job ahead of us— to change the world's opinion about us.

> We need a commitment to truth.
> We need a commitment to integrity.
> We need to love one another.
> We need to help one another grow.

"By this all men will know that you are my disciples, if you love one another" (John 13:35). As we strive for truthfulness, it needs to be a daily decision—beginning with the small things.

We need to encourage one another to be faithful in our commitments and promises. May we serve our Lord with all our hearts so that He can say of us, "You were faithful in the little things; I will put you over great things."

Serving

What's in a Customer?

"The only difference between stores is the way they treat their customers," reads a poster in a Nordstrom store. Nordstrom doesn't have customers, they have fans.

A recent study by Technical Assistance Research Programs (TARP), a research firm in Washington, D.C., shows that most customers won't complain to management if something goes wrong with their purchase, but, depending on the severity of the problem, they tell between nine and sixteen friends and acquaintances of their bad experiences. Some 13 percent will tell more than twenty people. More than two out of three customers who receive poor service will never buy from that store again, and, worse, management will never know why.

The study showed, however, that 95 percent of dissatisfied customers will buy from the store again if their problems are solved quickly. Even better, they will each tell eight people of the situation's happy ending.

According to the White House Office of Consumer Affairs, the average business never hears about 96 percent of its unhappy customers. That means that for every complaint received, there were twenty-six not reported, and six were considered "serious."

Charles A. Walgreen, Sr., said, "Every customer is a guest in our store and should be treated as such."

While riding on a hotel bus recently I bumped into Jim Brown of World Vision International. He was planning a partners meeting at the Holiday Inn just across from their international headquarters in Monrovia, California. New owners had just purchased the hotel and had determined to keep all the hotel staff. They saw great potential in each one, potential that thus far had gone untapped.

Their service left no stone unturned. Every request was met with a smile. Even a passing comment of how nice it would be to have the seventy-two countries represented by their native flags prompted the owners to search far and wide. They located all seventy-two flags, purchased them, and had them flying proudly at the entrance as the attendees arrived.

Hotel meeting room names were replaced with names World Vision wanted, such as Bulgaria, France, Singapore, and so on. Furniture was rearranged to World Vision's taste, and World Vision pictures were hung as a special touch in the meeting room.

If you had been the customer, would you have felt important? Would you have felt cared for? We can learn something here. Hotels have a good reason to try to please you: they want you to come back. We have an even better reason: our rewards are eternal.

Our customers, our clients, our donors, our members, our students, our parishioners are the lifeblood of any organization. Without them, there would be no organization. How they are treated has a direct effect on the success of our organizations.

We are admonished in Scripture to love and honor one another. That's the core of human relations, isn't it?

Stay Off Center Stage

At a conference hosted by the Christian Management Association, we had the privilege of hearing Lloyd Ogilvie, senior pastor of the First Presbyterian Church of Hollywood and the speaker on the radio program "Let God Love You." He told a story about a support actor who continually tried to steal the limelight from the star of the show. Finally, the director took him aside and grabbed him by the shoulders and said, "Listen, you're not the leading man—stop hugging center stage."

God shares His glory with no one. We need to move off center stage so that He can shine. "He must increase but I must decrease" (John 3:30, NASB).

As I left that conference I pondered those words—"stop hugging center stage." I began to reflect on God's provisions for me and for the organization where I have the privilege of serving. God has taken the inadequacies of this leader and has blessed, in spite of weaknesses, failures, and shortcomings. The growth that has come has been because of Him.

I began to realize just how little we can take credit for. No gifts or talents that we possess are because of our own doing—we have them only through God's mercy and grace. So if our gifts and talents are from Him, how can we boast of anything?

Even if we already know the answers to complex problems, we can't take the glory or honor. We know that God gave us the gifts we have. Everything that we have is a gift from Him. Isn't it humbling to realize how insignificant we are apart from Him?

I marveled the other day as I saw one of my colleagues using our photocopy machine as a sorter after the printing was all completed. It was an unbelievable timesaver for a tedious project. As she described it to me, I got so confused that all I could do was trust the fact that it could be done. I asked her how she had discovered that the machine could do it. She thought for a minute and said, "I really believe it was an inspiration from God. I knew collating these booklets was going to take forever, so I said, 'Lord, there must be an easier way'—then it came to me."

Our God is awesome. He takes our failures and shortcomings and makes something good out of them. He is interested in the little things and the big things.

Sometimes when I *feel* inadequate I realize that I actually *am* inadequate. But He is there to provide the inspiration and solutions to the most difficult situations.

We have a responsibility to develop the gifts and talents He has given us, in ourselves and in our staff, and to use them for His glory in His kingdom.

How important it is for us to move off center stage so that God can be glorified and so that those who are in our employment can receive acknowledgment for God's work through them.

"Let your light so shine before men, that they may see your good deeds and praise your Father in heaven" (Matthew 5:16).

As I flew at 30,000 feet above the clouds, pondering His glory, my heart was tender as I not only realized how truly inadequate I was apart from Him, but how magnificent He is. He is a God of mercy and a God of grace.

The chorus to the song we sing in church, "Our God Is an Awesome God," by Rich Mullins, floods my soul, and I affirm that our God truly is awesome (Psalm 68:35).

Servant Leadership— A Contradiction in Terms?

You've probably seen the little sign in a manager's office: "Lead, follow, or get out of the way!"

What is "leadership" anyway? Jesus said, "Whoever wants to be great among you must be your servant" (Matthew 20:26). Servant leadership—it seems to be a contradiction in terms. Jesus indicates that it isn't the way we usually think of things. It was a new, radical idea.

Jesus Made It Work

In the eyes of the world He was a nobody, the son of a tradesman. As God He *could* have taken over. But He *chose* not to. How did He lead?

1. *He knew where He was going.* He had a sense of direction. He set and clarified goals. How did He do that? Partly, at least, because He was well versed in Scripture and had a strong discipline of prayer.
2. *He communicated effectively.* He used familiar terms, clear illustrations. He spoke plainly but lovingly. He made clear the kind of behavior He was looking for. Training His followers was one of His highest priorities. He didn't just tell them what to do; He showed them.
3. *He provided for their needs.* He who had nothing of this world's goods found ways to provide what was needed for the work to continue.

4. *He gave Himself to them, in life and in death.* He took on the role of a servant and washed their feet, and told them (and us) to do the same.

5. *He "got out of the way" at the appropriate time.* Jesus, limited by human flesh, could only be one place at a time. The Spirit of God, indwelling believers, can be thousands of places.

I'm Trying to Make It Work!

What does all of that look like "in shoe leather"? I'm only beginning to learn, but here are some things that have occurred to me lately:

1. *I must place a high priority on thinking through the mission of the organization.* Through prayer, Bible study, good advice, and using the brains God gave me, I need to chart a clear course.

2. *I need to improve my communication skills.* How many times have I been irritated by a bank clerk or service station attendant who didn't know what she/he was doing? But what about God's ministry? Am I letting the staff know in detail what I expect? In my busy schedule of travel, appointments, and rushing about, I find that I am often not as careful to take quality time to nurture the management team as I should be. Returning from a trip to a desk filled with work can cause me to forget my human resource priorities. Am I willing to spend the time (and money) it takes to do the job well?

3. *Have I "counted the cost" of what I am attempting?* Am I frustrating staff members by expecting them to produce without the tools and resources they need? Am I a good steward of the resources I have?

4. *Am I willing to sacrifice for the staff?* To figuratively (maybe literally) wash their feet? After all, they are the ones actually *doing* the ministry. Is my ego so out of control that they must constantly bow to me? Do they understand how important they really are to the ministry? Do I take time regularly to praise (but not flatter) them?

5. *Do I know how to get out of the way?* As I do my management by walking around, I have a tendency to stick my two cents in where it isn't asked for. For me it's a discipline to let the staff solve problems without my interference. Am I willing to give them room to fail and to learn? (Aren't you glad God gives *us* room to fail?)

I confess, I've got a long way to go. But through God's grace I want to learn more about being a "servant leader."

Taking It on the Chin

I once read in a magazine, "Just in case you find any mistakes in this magazine, please remember they were put there for a purpose. We try to offer something for everyone. Some people are always looking for mistakes, and we didn't want to disappoint you."

Flattery is false positive feedback. It is destructive because it tells people to continue what they are doing when what they are doing is harmful. Negative feedback is corrective, because it tells us to stop doing something that is harmful.

We should seek criticism and welcome it, if it is honest and balanced. O. A. Bautista says, "One of the surest marks of good character is a person's ability to accept personal criticism without malice to the one who gives it."

In Matthew 7:3 we are asked, "And why do you look at the speck that is in your brother's eye, but do not notice the log that is in your own eye?" (NASB). Before we are able to give positive criticism, we must be able to recognize our own shortcomings and accept constructive feedback.

Criticism is more easily accepted when it is given by one who has earned the right to give it. We find correction easier to receive when we know we are loved and cared for by someone who has our best interest at heart.

We should cultivate an atmosphere where people feel free to give and receive constructive criticism. We should reward those who give us corrective feedback. A genuine "thank you" goes a long way.

We can invite constructive feedback by asking, "What can I do to improve this?" But we need to be ready for the answer that such a question invites. Becoming defensive, for example, would be highly inappropriate.

Failure is seldom fatal unless it is perpetuated by unwillingness to accept it. Michael Korda says, "The freedom to fail is vital if you're going to succeed. Most successful men and women fail time and time again, and it is a measure of their strength that failure merely propels them into some new attempt at success."[8]

Receiving only positive feedback would be like a furnace that is miswired so that the warmer it gets, the more heat it turns out. Eventually the house would burn down.

A healthy relationship is like a correctly wired thermostat that indicates, "Enough—stop!" Florence Littauer says, "Pruning is not punishment but purposeful planning."

When giving criticism we have to realize that it takes strong self-confidence to be able to receive constructive criticism well. Corrective feedback is more easily accepted if it is preceded by genuine praise. Peter Drucker has said that we should give nine praises before we have the right to give one criticism. How are your ratios?

My brother once said that before we have the right to bring correction—especially when someone is functioning outside of God's will—we should be so tender ourselves that we come nearly in tears.

Chris Lyons says, "Always keep your criticism up to date." Too often we make statements about others or harbor impressions that are no longer valid. God is in the business of changing people, and we are constantly growing and learning through His grace.

When we are falsely accused, it is healthy to realize that life balances out—many times we have deserved criticism but for some reason were spared.

When we criticize we should also take responsibility to offer assistance in making changes possible. An employee is criticized for substandard work, but his or her workload is so overwhelming that improvement is impossible. Criticism without assistance will only lead to increased frustration.

It is helpful when our constituents make suggestions on ways to improve our programs, and it is especially helpful when they suggest alternatives or volunteer to be part of the process to make change. Abraham Lincoln said, "He has a right to criticize who has a heart to help."

May we pray that God will give us the willingness to accept constructive criticism and the resolve to look for good in others so that we become proficient in honest praising.

The Privilege of Serving

I worked for a church some years ago, and every morning when I came to work a wonderful woman named Jane Fisher greeted me with a warm smile and a caring and loving spirit. The mere sight of her lifted my spirits. What a gift she had! She was the receptionist and loved her job. She considered it her calling to cheer everyone else up.

Jane was one of those individuals who couldn't wait to get to work in the morning. She did not consider herself "just a receptionist." She knew she was called of God to be the first person anyone met when he or she entered the door of the church office, and the first and sometimes only voice people heard when they called the church. What a magnificent public relations ambassador she was, and she didn't even know it. It was just a natural flow of love from her life.

Jane understood that the Lord didn't burden us with work; He blessed us with it. It is a privilege to serve Him each day of our lives.

Leadership is not control and domination of others. It is a choice opportunity to guide, encourage, and help others to be productive and successful. It is a spiritual ministry.

Leaders need to put people into the right positions so that they can perform well. The average person uses only 6 to 9 percent of his or her potential. What a challenge to tap into those hidden capabilities.

We need to look for new ways to keep people motivated. Peter Drucker suggests that we find a new challenge or a new position within the organization for those in our care every two years. He also says that a new employee should be reevaluated within six months of employment to determine his or her level of comfort within the job assignment.

I often use a personality test for employees. Sometimes after reviewing the results, we find that we need to have staff members swap jobs. The changes bring fresh challenges to both individuals as they tackle new assignments.

Since we spend so much of our time at work, job satisfaction is essential. It seems clear throughout Ecclesiastes that God wants us to have satisfaction in our work. For example, "Then I realized that it is good and proper for a man to eat and drink, and to find satisfaction in his toilsome labor under the sun during the few days of life God has given him—for this is his lot" (Ecclesiastes 5:18). And to "be happy in his work—this is a gift of God" (v. 19). Ecclesiastes 8:15 further says, "Then joy will accompany him in his work all the days of the life God has given him under the sun." It is exciting to know that the Lord does want us to find joy in our work for Him. Is your enjoyment employment?

The late Robert A. Cook said, "Hard work is a thrill and a joy when you are in the will of God." With hard work, we can also receive peaceful rest at the close of each day. There is nothing better than to know you have worked hard, you have run the race and completed the project and enjoyed the process.

Tom Phillips, president of Phillips Publishing, said his growth from a kitchen-table operation with revenues of $300,000 in 1974 to $40 million in 1989 was based on hiring the right people. "We hire bright, enthusiastic, aggressive and 'growable' people," he said. "And as these people grow, both personally and professionally, our company grows."

God in the
Workplace

Prayer,
the Key that Unlocks the Door

Jesus told us to pray always and not to give up (Luke 18:1). In 1 Thessalonians 5:17, Paul encourages us to "pray without ceasing" (NASB). In Psalm 55:17 we read, "Evening, morning and noon, I cry out in distress, and he hears my voice." The Bible is a book about prayer. Out of 667 recorded prayers, there are 454 recorded answers. God desires to show "great and unsearchable things you do not know" (Jeremiah 33:3). What an exciting invitation!

And yet at times prayer seems hard. We get caught up in the many "activities" of the day that keep us from the very thing that God has commanded us to do "without ceasing." Fortunately, He doesn't have set rules for prayer, and as we pray without ceasing we can pray at our desk, on our way to work, as we lie in bed in the morning ready to start the day, or on our knees. Prayer is wide open as to when, where, and how.

A friend of mine who is a nurse has found herself in an attitude of prayer because of several specific needs in her life. As she goes through the day, she finds that her mind is in a state of prayer. During one of her busy days of calling patients with test results, she left a message on one of the patient's machines instructing him what medicine was needed and where he should pick it up. At the end of the message instead of saying, "Good-bye," to her surprise, she said, "Amen."

Of course she was completely embarrassed, but isn't it inspiring that she had such an attitude of prayer that a normal message ended with "amen" rather than "good-bye"?

Prayer takes discipline. For a "Type A" personality such as myself, thoughts of the day's activities can quickly rush in to crowd out my concentration. As I struggled with this area of my life, I realized one way to help me center my concentration more effectively would be to write my prayers or even bang them out on the computer. It has been a wonderful avenue of discipline as I start each day. It also forces me into a regular pattern.

Oswald Chambers writes in *My Utmost for His Highest*,

> Prayer is an effort of will. After we have entered our secret place and have shut the door, the most difficult thing to do is to pray; we cannot get our minds into working order, and the first thing that conflicts is wandering thoughts. The great battle in private prayer is the overcoming of mental wool-gathering. We have to discipline our minds and concentrate on willful prayer.[9]

My husband and I have found that we can use our driving time or an evening walk to bring our concerns to the throne of grace.

Some years ago, the chairperson of the Christian Management Association board challenged me to begin having regular staff prayer time at the office. We took up the challenge and have made it a regular practice at the start of each day. Each staff person is assigned to lead prayer on a specific day. This also helps us all to participate directly in the prayer process. Additionally, we decided to take each day of the week and pray for a specific member's need.

I want God to show Himself strong and powerful. We need to clearly and genuinely admit our own insufficiencies and ask for His sufficiency. Without Him, we are nothing; with Him, we have the power and strength to serve Him.

It has been said, "Christians must get on their knees before they can get on their feet." The prayers we live on our feet are just as important as those we say on our knees.

My colleagues and I have been in the process of mobilizing prayer teams for our conferences. National board members, chapter leaders, chapters, staff, and so on are all praying for each person who will be attending the conferences. We pray that God will meet needs. We pray for each speaker as he or she prepares for the conference, that each one will sense God's specific leading for the workshop or keynote address. We pray for musicians, staff, and volunteers, for the hotel staff, for the weather, for the preparation process, and for other specific needs. We know the power of prayer and fully understand that we can do nothing apart from Him.

Without these prayer partners going before the Lord on our behalf, our efforts would all be in vain.

Management Technique Versus God's Wisdom

From time to time someone tells me that management expertise is unspiritual. They suggest that it is dangerous, even sinful. After all, we should depend on God's power, not man's wisdom.

On the surface, that's hard to argue with. Certainly we should obey God rather than man whenever the "wisdom" of man conflicts with the teaching of Scripture. But not all of man's learning is corrupt or perverted.

The Bible Doesn't Tell Us Everything We Need to Know!

Does that sound like heresy? Think for a moment. The Bible doesn't give us information that we could be expected to learn on our own. It doesn't tell us how to plant or cultivate crops (though it refers to those tasks). It does not even tell us how to have sex or birth babies. It presumes that we can figure it out or that such information will be passed on through other means.

The Bible is not meant to be comprehensive. It is not everything we need to know. But the Bible is authoritative. Where the Bible speaks we accept it as true even when it contradicts other teachings.

All Truth Is God's Truth

Since the creation is orderly and God has blessed us with eyes, ears, and minds (talk about a miracle!) we are able to observe the world around us and discover what works and what doesn't. Discovery is not sinful. In fact, it is foolish and shortsighted to fail to learn from our surroundings.

Nor is it wrong to learn from others. Even those outside the faith have eyes, ears, and minds. They too are capable of discovery and learning.

Whatever is true in the creation harmonizes perfectly with revealed truth in the Bible. They both come from the same source! When conflicts appear it is because we don't understand one or the other well enough.

Getting Rid of the "Versus"

The ideal Christian manager understands that what we learn from observation usually does not contradict what we learn from the Bible. He or she regards the Bible as authoritative but does not disregard other learning that speaks where the Bible is silent. We need to replace "versus" with "and."

I recently saw a good example of the "and" at work at the National Family Conference at Houston's Second Baptist Church. That enormous church has a staff of five hundred and literally thousands of volunteer workers. It functions smoothly and effectively because (1) they view the Bible as authoritative, (2) they have a clear vision of what they want to accomplish, (3) they use proved management techniques, and (4) they strive for excellence.

Ashes

Scene 1: Southern California. A woman stands beside a charred heap of rubble that until yesterday had been her beautiful home. She says, "We've lost everything we worked for." Her words haunt me. The sense of loss and futility she must be feeling overwhelm me. It would be hard to start again with absolutely nothing.

Scene 2: Heaven, one million years from now. Some will make the same statement: "I've lost everything I worked for."

Southern California's periodic fires can do unbelievable damage, but the Bible tells us that someday the entire earth will be destroyed by intense heat.

We need to choose how we invest our time with the same care that a builder must choose his materials. Believe it or not, many homes in fire-prone areas of Southern California are built with wood shake roofs. Wise builders now make roofs of materials that won't burn.

In 1 Corinthians 3 Paul talks about building upon the foundation Christ has laid. Some of our efforts are like building with materials that burn easily—wood, hay, and straw. When the fire comes, they become ashes. Much of our effort may be similarly transformed to worthless rubble, according to an eternal scale.

Others build with more costly but fireproof materials, such as gold, silver, and precious stones. These materials are expensive and difficult to work with, but they endure.

122

What has enduring value on an eternal scale? Actions that please God and bring others into His kingdom. Costly and precious acts of faith and obedience.

What most amazes me about Paul's analogy is that those who build foolishly and those who build wisely can both be Christians because they are all building on the foundation of Jesus Christ.

We can see that around us. We see people working hard for the cause of Christ but doing little good. Some actually may be doing more harm than good because they use up time and resources in tasks that are of little lasting value.

We see, for example, a church worker so busy with important committee meetings and projects that his or her family is ignored and there is no time to share Christ with neighbors. A fund-raiser successfully completes a campaign to support a "ministry," but the work is of questionable eternal value.

Sometimes we get trapped on the treadmill because we're too busy to think, to ask the hard questions. Someone puts a goal in front of us, and we go for it, never pausing to ask, "Is this really worthwhile?" or, "Is this God's priority for me right now?"

Often we do things for the sake of tradition. Perhaps there was a good reason for doing it once, long ago. But now the value of the action is never even questioned, just assumed. The person who is too busy to reflect on the ultimate value of what she or he is doing is probably building wooden structures in a fire zone.

Success by God's Standards

At a Chicago hotel in 1923, a group of powerful and successful businessmen met. The group consisted of the presidents of a leading steel manufacturer, the largest utility company, the New York Stock Exchange, Bank of International Settlements, and even a member of the President's cabinet. Over the years, the success stories of those tycoons were told and retold in magazines and newspapers. Young people were encouraged to follow their examples, and it was no wonder. Collectively, that group of gentlemen controlled more wealth than there was in the United States Treasury.

Twenty-five years later things had changed. Charles Schwab, the president of Bethlehem Steel, spent the last five years of his life living on borrowed money—and died penniless. Richard Whitney, the president of the New York Stock Exchange, spent time in Sing Sing. Leon Fraser, the president of the Bank of International Settlement, committed suicide. Ivan Kreuger, head of the world's greatest monopoly, also killed himself. Albert Fall, the member of the President's cabinet, was pardoned from prison so that he could die at home.

Those men learned how to make money, but they never learned how to live successfully. They were role models, but how many know of their unsuccessful ends?

We all have people in our lives whom we admire. We emulate them because of their success or influence. And sometimes, even if we are unaware of it, we are role models for others. The decisions we make, the friends we associate with, and the actions of our lives should reflect Christ living within us. We are being followed. Are we living exemplary lives so that we can be good role models? If we are following others, are we following those who are living successful lives by God's standards?

I remember that as my daughter, Lisa, was growing up, there were times when we would observe words or actions that she had picked up from her father or from me. She was our little mimic. At times the things she mimicked were not necessarily things we were proud of. We began to watch our actions and words more carefully.

Whether we are leading or following, we must obey Christ's example. He brought the truth to the marketplace, and so should we.

In 1 Peter 5:3 we are encouraged to serve eagerly, "not lording it over those entrusted to you, but being examples to the flock. And when the Chief Shepherd appears, you will receive the crown of glory that will never fade away."

The rewards for exemplary living cannot be measured by the world's standards—only God's. "Let your light shine before men, that they may see your good deeds and praise your Father in heaven" (Matthew 5:16).

Conclusion:
Excellence in Management

Excellence is a high cost item. The high cost is attention to detail when no one is looking. It takes time, energy, and attention. It isn't easy or natural. It is hard, disciplined work—not running around in a frenzy. It often means working long hours when others are reading and relaxing with their favorite novel. Excellence is being able to stand straight and look people in the eye, knowing that you were honest and gave it your all.

Ted Engstrom says, "Excellence is not an act, but a habit—it is a measurement." Good habits need to be developed by the entire team. For many of us it doesn't come automatically. We need to be constantly reminded of the importance of giving attention to every detail.

Bringing Out the Best in Your Team

Do you expect excellence from your team? A study was done some years ago by Robert Rosenthal and Lenore Jacobson, who asked the question, "Do some children perform poorly in school because their teachers expect them to?" At the beginning of the academic year new teachers were casually given the names of a few pupils who had exceptional learning ability. The teachers were told that tests had revealed that they were exceptional pupils and to expect them to be high performers throughout the year. In actuality, the names had been chosen at random.

The children were retested at the end of the school year with astonishing results. The "exceptional" children had gained as many as fifteen to twenty-seven IQ points from previous testing. Teachers indicated that those children were happier, more curious, more affectionate than average, and had a better chance of success in later years. The only change that had taken place was the attitude of the teachers.

Because the teachers had been led to expect more from the students, those students may have come to expect more of themselves.

Are we expecting the most from our staff, or do we expect them to blunder every project? If our expectations are low, we may be programming them for failure rather than success.

The One Minute Manager suggests that we "catch them doing something right"[10] and then, without waiting, praise them then and there.

Emphasize the Positive

It is difficult to be around negative people, and it's exhilarating to associate with positive, successful people. We need associates who stimulate our thinking and are encouragers rather than discouragers. We may need to distance ourselves from the pessimistic people who pull us down.

You have heard the phrase "garbage in, garbage out." We read another variation in Proverbs 23:7, "As he thinks within himself, so he is" (NASB). So the more negative phrases we either say or hear, the more difficult it is for us to have a positive attitude about ourselves and others.

As we strive for excellence, we may stumble and fall. As our colleagues strive for excellence, they may also fail. We need to be positive encouragers, forgiving one another in love and helping each other to develop good habits and practices that will bring about excellence in our tasks.

Let's motivate our staff, bring out the best in them, and together serve the Lord with all our hearts so He can say of us, "Well done, good and faithful servant."

Notes

1. E. M. Houtz, *Desk Top Devotion* (Colorado Springs: NavPress, 1989), p. 58.
2. Chuck Swindoll, *The Quest for Character* (Portland: Multnomah, 1987), p. 163.
3. Kenneth Blanchard and Spencer Johnson, *The One Minute Manager* (New York: Berkeley, 1982), p. 38.
4. Ibid., p. 44.
5. Ibid., p. 64.
6. David Schwartz, *The Magic of Thinking Big* (New York: Prentice-Hall, 1965).
7. "When Employees Turn into Thieves," *U.S. News and World Report*, September 26, 1983, pp. 79-80.
8. Michael Korda, *Success!* (New York: Random, 1977).
9. Oswald Chambers, *My Utmost for His Highest* (New York: Dodd, Mead, 1935), pp. 172.
10. Blanchard and Johnson, p. 38.

Moody Press, a ministry of the Moody Bible Institute,
is designed for education, evangelization, and edification.
If we may assist you in knowing more about Christ
and the Christian life, please write us without obligation:
Moody Press, c/o MLM, Chicago, Illinois 60610.